The Seven Pillars of Achievement
"Unveiling the Blueprint for Success"

DR. LESTER G. REID

"Success isn't built overnight; it's the culmination of dedication, perseverance, consistency and the unwavering support of the Seven Pillars of Achievement."

The Author of Amazon Best Sellers Books and #1 Hot New Releases: Maximizing Puts and Calls Options, Choosing Your Career Path, Mastering Financial Accounting, Maximizing Higher Education and Problem-Based Learning.

COPYRIGHT

The contents of this book, including but not limited to text, images, and illustrations, are protected under the copyright laws of United States of America and international conventions. The author and publisher have made every effort to ensure that the information provided Together is accurate and up to date at the time of publication.

Unauthorized reproduction or distribution of any part of this book is prohibited. This includes but is not limited to copying, scanning, or distributing in any form or by any means, including electronic, mechanical, photocopying, recording, or otherwise, without the prior written permission of the author and publisher.

Copyright © 2024

by

Dr. Lester Reid

ISBN: 978 -1-7340601-8-8

Publishing Company

Global Higher Education Institute Publishing.

ACKNOWLEDGEMENT

As I reflect on the completion of this book, **"The Seven Pillars of Achievement: Unveiling the Blueprint for Success,"** I am filled with gratitude for the support and contributions of numerous individuals who have played pivotal roles in its realization.

First and foremost, I extend my deepest appreciation to my family for their unwavering love, encouragement, and understanding throughout this journey. Your constant support has been my anchor, enabling me to pursue this endeavor with passion and dedication.

To my colleagues and friends who have provided feedback, encouragement, and inspiration along the way, I extend my heartfelt thanks. Your diverse perspectives and shared experiences have enriched the narrative, making this book a true reflection of collective wisdom and collaboration.

I also extend my appreciation to the you and supporters of my previous works, whose enthusiasm and feedback have motivated me to continue exploring new horizons and sharing insights on personal and professional development.

I am deeply grateful for the unwavering support of my family, whose love and encouragement have been my guiding force. To my colleagues and friends, your feedback and inspiration have shaped this book into a testament of collective wisdom. I also extend my appreciation to my readers and supporters, whose enthusiasm propels me forward. Lastly, to all those committed to personal and professional growth, may "The Seven Pillars of Achievement" illuminate your path to success and fulfillment. Together, let us continue to strive for excellence and embrace the journey of continuous growth and empowerment.

ABOUT THIS BOOK

"In 'The Seven Pillars of Achievement: *Unveiling the Blueprint for Success,"* you are invited on a transformative journey toward personal and professional fulfillment. Through a comprehensive framework comprising seven essential pillars, this book offers invaluable insights and practical strategies for navigating the complexities of the achievement journey.

At its core lies the crucial first pillar: **Identification.** You are encouraged to develop a keen sense of observation and proactive mindset to recognize hidden challenges and opportunities. From there, the journey progresses to the second pillar: **Action,** where aspirations are translated into tangible results through strategic execution.

Continuing the ascent, you immerse into the third pillar: **Education,** which emphasizes the importance of continuous learning and knowledge acquisition in overcoming obstacles. The fourth pillar, **Application,** demonstrates how to effectively apply newfound insights to real-world situations, fostering progress and innovation.

Acknowledgment and appreciation take center stage in the fifth and sixth pillars, respectively. You are reminded of the significance of: **Appreciation,** recognizing efforts and **Compensation,** rewarding contributions, cultivating a supportive environment conducive to growth and success.

Finally, the journey culminates in the seventh pillar: **Celebration.** Here, you are encouraged to savor the fruits of their labor, fostering a sense of accomplishment and renewal as they reflect on their achievements.

Through practical guidance and inspiring anecdotes, **"The Seven Pillars of Achievement"** equips you with the tools and mindset needed to embark on their own journey toward success. Whether navigating personal goals or organizational challenges, this book serves as a beacon of guidance and inspiration for all those striving to unlock their full potential.

PREFACE

In a world filled with endless possibilities and opportunities, achieving success can often feel like navigating a labyrinth without a map. It's easy to become overwhelmed by the complexities of our goals and aspirations, unsure of where to begin or how to proceed.

This book is born out of a deep-seated belief in the power of intentional action and strategic thinking. Drawing from personal experiences, observations, and insights gathered over years of academic study and professional practice, I have crafted a roadmap—a blueprint—that aims to guide you through the intricacies of the achievement journey.

"The Seven Pillars of Achievement" is not just another self-help book offering generic advice. It is a meticulously crafted framework designed to equip you with the tools, mindset, and strategies necessary to overcome obstacles, seize opportunities, and ultimately realize your full potential.

Each pillar serves as a foundational element, building upon the last to create a solid structure upon which to construct your path to success. From the initial identification of challenges and opportunities to the joyous celebration of achievements, this book offers practical guidance and actionable insights every step of the way.

But beyond mere instruction, this book is an invitation—an invitation to embark on a journey of self-discovery, growth, and transformation. It is an invitation to challenge the status quo, to push beyond your comfort zone, and to embrace the limitless possibilities that await you.

As you examine the pages that follow, I encourage you to approach this journey with an open mind and a willingness to learn. Embrace the challenges, celebrate the victories, and above all, never lose sight of the incredible potential that lies within you.

I am deeply honored to accompany you on this journey, and I trust that **"The Seven Pillars of Achievement"** will serve as a guiding light, illuminating your path to success and fulfillment.

Table of Contents

CHAPTER ONE

Introduction

In the expansive terrain of personal and professional development, the concept of **"pillars"** stands as a beacon of guidance, illuminating the path toward success. These pillars represent the foundational principles, values, and practices that serve as the bedrock upon which individuals and organizations build their journeys of accomplishment. Just as sturdy pillars support the weight of a grand structure, these foundational elements uphold the aspirations and ambitions of those who seek to achieve greatness.

Pillars serve as the framework upon which individuals can construct their goals and aspirations. They provide a sense of direction and purpose, helping individuals navigate the complexities of life and work towards their desired outcomes with clarity and determination. Like a compass guiding traveler through uncharted territories, pillars offer guidance and support, empowering individuals to stay focused and resilient in the face of adversity.

Moreover, pillars serve as a source of inspiration and motivation, fueling individuals with the courage and confidence to pursue their dreams. By embodying values such as perseverance, resilience, and integrity, individuals can overcome obstacles and setbacks, emerging stronger and more determined to succeed. In this way, pillars act as catalysts for personal and professional growth, enabling individuals to reach new heights of achievement and fulfillment.

Additionally, pillars foster a sense of accountability and responsibility, encouraging individuals to take ownership of their actions and decisions. By aligning their behavior with their core values and principles, individuals can cultivate a sense of integrity and authenticity that resonates with others. This authenticity builds trust and credibility, creating opportunities for collaboration and collective achievement. Thus, pillars not only support individual success but also contribute to the growth and prosperity of communities and organizations.

Defining Pillars

At its essence, a pillar is more than just a structural component; it is a symbol of strength, resilience, and stability. In the context of personal and professional growth, pillars encompass a wide array of principles and practices that provide support and guidance along the journey toward success. These pillars may include values such as integrity, perseverance, and adaptability, as well as strategies like goal-setting, time management, and collaboration.

The concept of a pillar extends beyond its physical form. It embodies an idea of strength, resilience, and stability – qualities essential for navigating the twists and turns of personal and professional growth. When we speak of the "Defining Pillars" in the context of achievement, we examine the very essence of what sustains us on our journey towards success.

At the core of these pillars lie a myriad of principles and practices, each contributing to the sturdy framework upon which our aspirations stand. Integrity, for instance, serves as a foundational pillar, guiding our actions with honesty, ethics, and moral fortitude. It's the unwavering commitment to doing what is right, even when faced with challenges or temptations to compromise.

Perseverance stands tall as another vital pillar, representing the tenacity and determination required to overcome obstacles and setbacks. It's the resilience to keep pushing forward, even in the face of adversity, knowing that every setback is an opportunity for growth and learning. Without perseverance, dreams remain merely aspirations, never materializing into tangible achievements.

Adaptability emerges as a dynamic pillar, flexing and adjusting to the ever-changing landscapes of life and work. In a world marked by rapid technological advancements and shifting paradigms, the ability to adapt becomes paramount. Those who embrace change and remain agile are better equipped to thrive amidst uncertainty, turning challenges into opportunities for innovation and progress.

But beyond these foundational principles, the pillars of achievement also encompass practical strategies and techniques that empower individuals to reach their goals. Goal-setting, for instance, serves as a guiding beacon, providing direction and clarity amidst the chaos of daily life. By defining clear and measurable objectives, individuals can chart a course towards their desired outcomes, staying focused and motivated along the way.

Time management emerges as another crucial pillar, recognizing the finite nature of time and the importance of using it wisely. With competing demands vying for our attention, effective time management skills enable us to prioritize tasks, allocate resources efficiently, and strike a balance between work, leisure, and personal pursuits. By mastering the art of time management, individuals can maximize productivity and minimize stress, unlocking their full potential.

Collaboration, too, stands as a pillar of achievement, acknowledging the power of synergy and teamwork in accomplishing shared goals. In an interconnected world, success often hinges on the ability to collaborate effectively with others, leveraging diverse perspectives, skills, and resources. By fostering a spirit of collaboration, individuals can amplify their impact, achieving more together than they ever could alone.

As we reflect on the defining pillars of achievement, we come to realize that they are not merely abstract concepts but guiding principles that shape our actions, attitudes, and aspirations. They form the bedrock upon which we build our dreams and ambitions, providing the support and stability needed to weather life's storms and soar to new heights of success.

In the journey towards achievement, let us embrace these pillars as beacons of hope and inspiration, guiding us forward with clarity, courage, and conviction. For it is through our commitment to these principles and practices that we transform our aspirations into reality, fulfilling our potential and leaving a lasting legacy of accomplishment for generations to come.

The Role of Pillars

Pillars play a critical role in the pursuit of achievement. They serve as guiding principles, providing individuals and organizations with a roadmap for navigating challenges, overcoming obstacles, and reaching their desired destinations. Just as a ship relies on a compass to chart its course through uncharted waters, individuals rely on pillars to steer them toward their goals with clarity and purpose.

Moreover, pillars offer a sense of stability and consistency in an ever-changing world. In times of uncertainty or adversity, they serve as reliable anchors, grounding individuals in their values and beliefs and providing a sense of direction amidst chaos. Like the steady hand of a navigator guiding a ship through a storm, pillars help individuals weather the challenges they encounter on their journey toward success.

In the intricate tapestry of human endeavor, pillars emerge as indispensable guides, illuminating the path to achievement with clarity and purpose. These steadfast principles not only provide direction but also serve as beacons of stability and resilience in a world marked by uncertainty and change. As we explore the critical role of pillars in the pursuit of success, we uncover their profound impact on individuals and organizations alike.

At its core, the role of pillars is akin to that of a compass, guiding individuals through the complexities of life's journey. Just as a ship relies on its compass to navigate uncharted waters, individuals rely on pillars to steer them toward their goals with unwavering determination. These guiding principles, whether rooted in integrity, perseverance, or adaptability, offer a roadmap for navigating challenges and overcoming obstacles along the way.

Moreover, pillars serve as pillars of stability and consistency amidst the turbulence of an ever-changing world. In times of uncertainty or adversity, they stand as reliable anchors, grounding individuals in their values and beliefs and providing a sense of direction amidst chaos. Like the steady hand of a navigator guiding a ship through a storm, pillars help individuals weather the challenges they encounter on their journey toward success.

Consider, for instance, the role of integrity as a guiding pillar. In a world fraught with moral dilemmas and ethical quandaries, integrity serves as a steadfast compass, guiding individuals to uphold their principles and do what is right, even in the face of temptation or adversity. By adhering to principles of honesty, trustworthiness, and moral courage, individuals cultivate a reputation for reliability and integrity, laying the foundation for enduring success and fulfillment.

Similarly, perseverance emerges as a pivotal pillar in the pursuit of achievement. In the face of setbacks and obstacles, it is perseverance that fuels the fires of determination, driving individuals to press onward in the pursuit of their goals. Whether facing rejection, failure, or seemingly insurmountable challenges, those who embody the spirit of perseverance refuse to be deterred, drawing strength from their resilience and unwavering resolve.

Adaptability, too, plays a critical role as a pillar of achievement, particularly in an era defined by rapid technological advancements and shifting socio-economic landscapes. Those who embrace change and remain agile are better equipped to thrive amidst uncertainty, turning challenges into opportunities for growth and innovation. By cultivating a mindset of flexibility and adaptability, individuals can navigate change with confidence, seizing new opportunities and charting new pathways to success.

Moreover, pillars foster a sense of community and collaboration, uniting individuals and organizations in pursuit of shared goals and aspirations. By fostering a spirit of cooperation and mutual support, pillars create an environment where diverse perspectives are valued, and collective achievements are celebrated. In a world marked by interconnectedness and interdependence, collaboration emerges as a powerful catalyst for innovation and progress, driving individuals and organizations to greater heights of achievement than they could ever reach alone.

In essence, the role of pillars in the pursuit of achievement is critical and profound. They serve as guiding lights, offering clarity and direction amidst life's uncertainties. They provide stability and resilience, anchoring individuals in their values and beliefs. And they foster collaboration and community, uniting individuals in pursuit of shared goals and aspirations. As we harness the power of these pillars, we unlock the potential for transformative growth and enduring success, both personally and professionally.

Types of Pillars

Pillars come in many shapes and forms, each serving a unique purpose in the pursuit of achievement. Some pillars may be personal, such as self-discipline, resilience, and self-awareness, while others may be professional, such as leadership, innovation, and collaboration. Regardless of their specific nature, all pillars share a common goal: to empower individuals to reach their full potential and achieve their aspirations.

In the intricate tapestry of human endeavor, pillars emerge as the foundational building blocks that support the edifice of achievement. These pillars, diverse in nature and purpose, serve as guiding beacons, illuminating the path to success with clarity and purpose. As we explore the myriad types of pillars that contribute to personal and professional growth, we uncover their profound impact on individuals and organizations alike.

At the heart of the myriad types of pillars lie those that are deeply personal, shaping the very essence of who we are and how we navigate the world. Self-discipline stands tall as one such pillar, embodying the capacity to exert control over one's impulses and actions in pursuit of long-term goals. It's the ability to stay focused, motivated, and committed, even in the face of distractions or temptations. By cultivating self-discipline, individuals harness the power to transform aspirations into reality, fostering a sense of empowerment and achievement.

Resilience emerges as another indispensable pillar of personal growth, embodying the ability to bounce back from adversity, setbacks, and challenges. In a world marked by uncertainty and change, resilience serves as a shield, protecting individuals from the debilitating effects of failure or disappointment. Those who embody the spirit of resilience are better equipped to weather life's storms, emerging stronger and more resilient with each trial they endure.

Self-awareness, too, stands as a pillar of personal growth, offering individuals insight into their own strengths, weaknesses, and motivations. It's the ability to introspect, reflect, and understand oneself on a deeper level, paving the way for personal growth and development. By cultivating self-awareness, individuals gain clarity of purpose and direction, aligning their actions with their values and aspirations.

In the realm of professional achievement, a distinct set of pillars comes into play, guiding individuals and organizations towards success in their chosen fields. Leadership stands as a cornerstone pillar, embodying the ability to inspire, motivate, and influence others towards a common goal. Whether leading a team, a project, or an entire organization, effective leadership is essential for driving innovation, fostering collaboration, and achieving sustainable growth.

Innovation emerges as another critical pillar of professional achievement, fueling progress and driving organizational success in an increasingly competitive marketplace. Those who embrace a spirit of innovation are better positioned to adapt to changing market dynamics, anticipate customer needs, and seize new opportunities for growth and expansion. By fostering a culture of innovation, organizations can stay ahead of the curve, remaining agile and responsive to emerging trends and technologies.

Collaboration, too, stands as a pillar of professional achievement, recognizing the power of teamwork and cooperation in achieving shared goals and objectives. In a world marked by interconnectedness and interdependence, effective collaboration is essential for driving organizational success and achieving sustainable growth. By fostering a culture of collaboration, organizations can harness the collective talents and expertise of their workforce, unlocking new opportunities for innovation, creativity, and success.

As we reflect on the diverse types of pillars that contribute to personal and professional achievement, we come to realize their profound impact on individuals and organizations alike. Whether personal or professional in nature, these pillars serve as the bedrock upon which aspirations are built, empowering individuals to reach their full potential and achieve their highest aspirations. As we harness the power of these pillars, we unlock the potential for transformative growth and enduring success, both personally and professionally.

Understanding Achievement

At its core, achievement is the culmination of effort, determination, and perseverance. It is the realization of goals, aspirations, and dreams, reflecting the progress and growth that individuals experience on their journey through life. Achievements can take many forms, ranging from academic and career milestones to personal victories and contributions to society.

At the very heart of the human experience lies the concept of achievement – a testament to the boundless potential and indomitable spirit that resides within each of us. It is the realization of goals, the fulfillment of aspirations, and the embodiment of dreams, reflecting the progress and growth that mark our journey through life. In delving deeper into the essence of achievement, we uncover its critical nature and profound significance in shaping our individual and collective destinies.

Achievement, at its core, is a testament to the power of effort, determination, and perseverance. It is the result of countless hours of hard work, sacrifice, and unwavering commitment to a vision or goal. Whether scaling the heights of academic excellence, pursuing a fulfilling career, or making meaningful contributions to society, achievement is the tangible expression of our innate drive to strive for excellence and make a positive impact on the world around us.

Yet, achievements are not confined to grandiose feats or monumental milestones. They can take many forms, ranging from the seemingly mundane to the extraordinary, from the personal to the collective. For some, achievement may manifest as academic accolades, professional advancements, or entrepreneurial endeavors – tangible markers of success that garner recognition and acclaim. For others, achievement may be found in the quiet moments of personal growth, the triumphs over adversity, or the acts of kindness and compassion that leave an indelible mark on the lives of others.

Indeed, understanding achievement requires us to look beyond the surface and recognize the inherent value of every individual journey. It is not solely about reaching the summit of a mountain or crossing the finish line of a race, but rather about the growth, learning, and transformation that occur along the way. Each step taken, each obstacle overcome, and each lesson learned contributes to the rich tapestry of our achievements, shaping us into the people we are meant to become.

Moreover, achievement is deeply intertwined with the concept of progress – the ongoing journey of self-discovery and self-improvement that propels us forward in pursuit of our goals and aspirations. It is a dynamic process characterized by resilience, adaptability, and a willingness to embrace change. As we strive towards our objectives, we inevitably encounter challenges, setbacks, and detours along the way. Yet, it is through these experiences that we grow stronger, more resilient, and more capable of overcoming whatever obstacles may lie in our path.

Importantly, achievement is not solely an individual endeavor but also a collective one – shaped by the support, guidance, and encouragement of others. Whether through mentorship, collaboration, or the collective efforts of a community, achievements are often the result of shared experiences and shared goals. In celebrating our own achievements, we also acknowledge the contributions of those who have helped us along the way – teachers who have imparted knowledge, mentors who have offered guidance, and loved ones who have provided unwavering support.

In essence, understanding achievement is about recognizing the inherent potential that lies within each of us and embracing the journey of growth, progress, and self-discovery that unfolds before us. It is about setting ambitious goals, overcoming obstacles, and striving to become the best version of ourselves. And ultimately, it is about making a meaningful impact on the world around us – leaving a legacy of inspiration, resilience, and hope for generations to come.

The Journey of Achievement

The journey of achievement is a dynamic and ever-evolving process, shaped by the interplay of various factors, including individual goals, external circumstances, and internal motivations. It is a journey marked by highs and lows, successes and setbacks, but ultimately, it is a journey of growth and self-discovery.

Boarding on the journey of achievement is akin to setting sail on an ocean of possibilities, where the winds of ambition propel us forward towards the distant shores of our aspirations. It is a dynamic and ever-evolving process, shaped by the interplay of various factors, including individual goals, external circumstances, and internal motivations. As we navigate the twists and turns of this voyage, we encounter highs and lows, successes and setbacks, but ultimately, it is a journey of growth and self-discovery that transforms us in profound ways.

At the outset of our journey, we set our sights on the horizon, envisioning the destination that beckons us with its promise of fulfillment and accomplishment. Our goals, whether lofty or humble, serve as the guiding stars that illuminate our path, providing direction and purpose amidst the vast expanse of possibilities. With determination in our hearts and a spirit of adventure in our souls, we embark on our quest, eager to conquer the challenges that lie ahead.

Yet, as we journey forth, we soon come to realize that the path to achievement is not always smooth sailing. Along the way, we encounter storms that threaten to derail our progress, obstacles that seem insurmountable, and setbacks that test the very limits of our resolve. It is during these moments of trial and tribulation that our true strength is revealed – our ability to persevere in the face of adversity, to rise above our fears and doubts, and to forge ahead with unwavering determination.

But amidst the challenges, there are also moments of triumph – milestones reached, obstacles overcome, and goals achieved. These victories, whether big or small, serve as beacons of hope and inspiration, fueling our passion and renewing our sense of purpose. They remind us of the progress we have made and the potential that lies within us, propelling us ever onward towards our ultimate destination.

Yet, the journey of achievement is not just about reaching the summit; it is also about the lessons we learn and the growth we experience along the way. Each obstacle we overcome, each setback we face, and each victory we celebrate shapes us into the person we are meant to become. We learn resilience in the face of adversity, humility in moments of triumph, and gratitude for the blessings that grace our path.

Moreover, the journey of achievement is deeply intertwined with the concept of self-discovery – the process of uncovering our true passions, strengths, and values. As we navigate the challenges and opportunities that present themselves, we gain a deeper understanding of ourselves and our place in the world. We discover what truly matters to us, what inspires us, and what drives us to keep moving forward, even when the seas are rough.

Alongside our individual efforts, the journey of achievement is also shaped by the support and encouragement of those around us – our family, friends, mentors, and peers. Their guidance, wisdom, and encouragement serve as lifelines in moments of doubt and despair, reminding us that we are not alone in our quest for success.

The journey of achievement is a transformative odyssey that challenges us to grow, to persevere, and to discover the depths of our potential. It is a journey marked by highs and lows, successes and setbacks, but ultimately, it is a journey that leads us towards self-realization and fulfillment. As we navigate the seas of possibility, let us embrace the adventure with open hearts and steadfast resolve, knowing that every step we take brings us closer to our dreams.

The Interconnection of Pillars and Achievement

The relationship between pillars and achievement is symbiotic, each reinforcing and supporting the other in a continuous cycle of growth and development. Pillars provide the foundation upon which achievements are built, offering the structure and support necessary to sustain progress and overcome obstacles. In turn, achievements serve as validation of the effectiveness of these pillars, affirming their importance and relevance in the pursuit of success.

Understanding the role of pillars in the journey of achievement is essential for individuals and organizations alike. By recognizing the importance of these foundational principles and integrating them into their daily lives and practices, individuals can unlock their full potential and realize their aspirations. Whether personal or professional, the journey of achievement is guided by these pillars, serving as beacons of light in the pursuit of greatness.

In the grand tapestry of human endeavor, the relationship between pillars and achievement is not merely incidental but deeply intertwined, each influencing and complementing the other in a dance of synergy and support. Like the interlocking pieces of a puzzle, pillars provide the essential framework upon which achievements are built, offering the structure and stability necessary to navigate the twists and turns of the journey towards success. In turn, achievements serve as a testament to the efficacy of these pillars, validating their significance and reaffirming their role in the pursuit of greatness.

At the heart of this interconnection lies the recognition that pillars serve as the guiding principles that shape our actions, attitudes, and aspirations. Whether personal or professional in nature, these pillars embody a set of core values and beliefs that provide the moral and ethical compass by which we navigate the complexities of life. Integrity, for instance, stands as a pillar of unwavering honesty and ethical conduct, guiding individuals to uphold their principles and do what is right, even in the face of adversity. By adhering to principles of integrity, individuals cultivate trust, credibility, and respect, laying the foundation for meaningful achievements and lasting success.

Similarly, perseverance emerges as a pivotal pillar in the pursuit of achievement, embodying the resilience and determination to overcome obstacles and pursue goals with unwavering resolve. In the face of setbacks and challenges, it is perseverance that fuels the fires of determination, propelling individuals forward in their quest for excellence. By embodying the spirit of perseverance, individuals demonstrate a willingness to endure hardships, overcome setbacks, and stay the course in pursuit of their dreams.

Moreover, the relationship between pillars and achievement extends beyond mere individual endeavors to encompass the collective aspirations of organizations and communities. In the realm of professional achievement, for instance, pillars such as leadership, innovation, and collaboration serve as the cornerstone principles that drive organizational success and propel teams towards their goals. Effective leadership, characterized by vision, inspiration, and integrity, empowers teams to overcome obstacles, unleash their creativity, and achieve breakthrough results. Innovation, meanwhile, fuels progress and drives competitive advantage, enabling organizations to adapt to changing market dynamics and seize new opportunities for growth and expansion. And collaboration fosters a culture of teamwork and mutual support, uniting individuals towards a common purpose and amplifying their collective impact.

Yet, it is in the interplay between pillars and achievements that the true magic happens – where aspirations are transformed into reality, and dreams into tangible outcomes. Achievements serve as the ultimate validation of the effectiveness of these pillars, providing tangible evidence of their impact and relevance in the pursuit of success. Whether it's reaching a personal milestone, accomplishing a professional goal, or making a meaningful contribution to society, achievements serve as mile markers along the journey towards greatness, affirming the importance of the pillars that guided us along the way.

Essentially, the interconnection of pillars and achievement underscores the profound impact that these guiding principles have on our individual and collective destinies. By recognizing the symbiotic relationship between pillars and achievements and integrating them into our daily lives and practices, we can unlock our full potential and realize our highest aspirations. Whether charting a course towards personal fulfillment or driving organizational success, the journey of achievement is guided by these pillars, serving as beacons of light in the pursuit of greatness.

Pillar 1: Identification - Unveiling the Essence

At the heart of every significant achievement lies a critical process that serves as the foundation for success: identification. Like turning on a spotlight in a dark room, identification illuminates the contours of challenges or opportunities that demand attention. This initial pillar sets the stage for intentional and purposeful action, guiding individuals and organizations towards their goals. In this comprehensive exploration, we examine the critical nature of identification, its manifestations across various contexts, and its pivotal role in laying the groundwork for accomplishment.

Identification serves as the compass that guides individuals and organizations through the complexities of the achievement journey. It provides clarity amidst uncertainty, enabling stakeholders to navigate towards their objectives with confidence and conviction. Without a clear understanding of the challenges and opportunities that lie ahead, efforts towards progress may falter or veer off course. Therefore, the process of identification is not merely about recognizing what is visible on the surface; it requires a deeper understanding of underlying dynamics, motivations, and potential obstacles.

Furthermore, identification fosters a proactive mindset that empowers individuals and organizations to seize opportunities and overcome challenges. By staying attuned to changing market conditions, emerging trends, and shifting consumer preferences, stakeholders can position themselves for success in dynamic and competitive environments. This proactive approach enables individuals and organizations to stay ahead of the curve, anticipate challenges, and capitalize on opportunities before they arise.

Moreover, identification encourages innovation and creativity by encouraging stakeholders to think outside the box and explore unconventional solutions. By challenging the status quo and questioning assumptions, individuals and organizations can uncover new possibilities and drive transformative change. This spirit of innovation is essential for staying relevant and competitive in today's rapidly evolving landscape, where disruptive technologies and paradigm shifts are reshaping industries and markets.

Additionally, identification fosters a culture of accountability and responsibility within organizations, where stakeholders take ownership of their actions and decisions. By identifying areas for improvement and addressing shortcomings proactively, individuals and organizations can continuously strive for excellence and drive continuous improvement. This culture of accountability promotes transparency, integrity, and trust, laying the foundation for sustainable growth and long-term success.

Identification is not just a preliminary step in the achievement journey; it is the cornerstone upon which success is built. By illuminating the contours of challenges and opportunities, identification empowers individuals and organizations to chart a course towards their goals with clarity, purpose, and determination. In the following sections, we will explore the various manifestations of identification across different contexts and examine its transformative impact on personal and organizational achievement.

Understanding Identification

Identification, as the first pillar of achievement, encompasses a spectrum of activities that involve keen observation and proactive discernment. It is the process of uncovering what may be concealed beneath the surface, whether in personal aspirations, organizational challenges, or market dynamics. This heightened awareness goes beyond surface-level observations, enabling individuals and entities to discern the nuances of their environment and identify opportunities for growth or improvement.

Manifestations of Identification

In the realm of personal development, identification involves recognizing one's own goals, aspirations, strengths, and areas for improvement. It requires introspection and self-awareness, as individuals navigate their desires and ambitions to chart a path towards fulfillment.

In the context of business and entrepreneurship, identification takes on a strategic dimension. It entails identifying market gaps, emerging trends, consumer needs, and organizational challenges. This requires a deep understanding of market dynamics, competitor analysis, and industry trends to position oneself for success.

The Importance of Identification in Achievement

Identification serves as the catalyst for intentional and purposeful action. By acknowledging challenges or opportunities, individuals and organizations can move beyond complacency and take the first step towards accomplishment. It is about asking the right questions, being attuned to the needs of the environment, and possessing the courage to confront realities.

Moreover, identification lays a solid foundation for the subsequent pillars of achievement. Without a clear understanding of the challenges and opportunities at hand, efforts towards goal attainment may lack direction and purpose. Identification provides the clarity and focus necessary to navigate the complexities of the achievement journey.

Practical Strategies for Effective Identification

To effectively harness the power of identification, individuals and organizations can employ several strategies:

1. Cultivate self-awareness: Engage in reflection and introspection to gain insight

into personal goals, strengths, weaknesses, and aspirations.
2. Stay informed: Keep abreast of industry trends, market dynamics, and emerging opportunities through continuous learning and research.
3. Seek feedback: Solicit input from mentors, peers, and stakeholders to gain perspective and identify blind spots.
4. Embrace curiosity: Maintain a curious mindset that seeks to explore and understand the world around you, uncovering hidden opportunities and insights.
5. Take calculated risks: Be willing to step outside your comfort zone and pursue opportunities that align with your goals, even if they involve uncertainty or risk.

By incorporating these strategies into their approach, individuals and organizations can enhance their ability to identify opportunities for growth and achievement.

The Intersection of Identification and Personal Development

In the realm of personal development, identification plays a fundamental role in guiding individuals towards self-discovery and growth. It involves introspection, reflection, and a deep understanding of one's values, passions, strengths, and areas for improvement. By identifying personal goals and aspirations, individuals can align their actions and decisions with their overarching vision for success.

Furthermore, identification enables individuals to recognize limiting beliefs, negative patterns, and obstacles that may impede their progress. Through self-awareness and introspection, individuals can confront these challenges head-on, develop strategies for overcoming them, and cultivate resilience in the face of adversity.

Moreover, identification fosters a sense of purpose and direction, empowering individuals to pursue their passions and aspirations with clarity and conviction. By understanding their unique strengths and talents, individuals can leverage their capabilities to achieve meaningful goals and make a positive impact in their personal and professional lives.

The Intersection of Identification and Organizational Success

In the realm of business and entrepreneurship, identification is equally essential for organizational success. It involves identifying market opportunities, consumer needs, industry trends, and organizational challenges to position the company for growth and innovation.

Effective identification enables organizations to stay ahead of the curve, anticipate changes in the market, and capitalize on emerging opportunities. By understanding customer preferences, market dynamics, and competitive pressures, organizations can develop strategic initiatives that drive growth, profitability, and competitive advantage.

Moreover, identification is critical for organizational agility and adaptability in a rapidly evolving business landscape. By identifying potential threats and disruptions, organizations can proactively mitigate risks, capitalize on opportunities, and navigate uncertainties with confidence and resilience.

Furthermore, identification fosters a culture of innovation and continuous improvement within organizations. By encouraging employees to identify and address inefficiencies, bottlenecks, and opportunities for innovation, organizations can drive productivity, creativity, and operational excellence.

Case Studies: Real-World Examples of Effective Identification

To illustrate the importance of identification in achievement, let us examine a few real-world examples:

1. **Apple Inc.:** Apple's success can be attributed, in part, to its keen identification of

consumer needs and preferences. By recognizing the demand for user-friendly, aesthetically pleasing technology products, Apple has been able to develop innovative products that resonate with customers and drive market demand.

2. **Elon Musk and SpaceX:** Elon Musk's visionary leadership and strategic identification of market opportunities have been instrumental in the success of SpaceX. By identifying the growing demand for commercial space travel and satellite launches, Musk has positioned SpaceX as a leading player in the aerospace industry, driving innovation and technological advancement.

3. **Oprah Winfrey:** Oprah Winfrey's success as a media mogul can be attributed to her keen identification of audience preferences and interests. By understanding the needs and aspirations of her viewers, Winfrey has been able to develop programming that resonates with audiences, driving ratings, and ad revenue.

4. **Amazon:** Amazon's success stems from its adept identification of consumer preferences and market trends. Through data-driven analysis and customer feedback, Amazon continuously identifies emerging needs and opportunities, leading to the development of new products, services, and business ventures.

5. **Netflix:** Netflix revolutionized the entertainment industry by identifying the shift in consumer behavior towards streaming services. By recognizing the demand for on-demand content and personalized recommendations, Netflix has become a dominant player in the digital media landscape.

6. **Airbnb:** Airbnb identified the untapped potential in the hospitality industry by connecting travelers with unique accommodation options. By leveraging the sharing economy and identifying the desire for authentic travel experiences, Airbnb disrupted the traditional hotel industry and achieved rapid growth.

7. **Uber:** Uber transformed the transportation industry by identifying the need for convenient, on-demand ridesharing services. By recognizing the limitations of traditional taxi services and the growing demand for affordable transportation options, Uber revolutionized urban mobility.

8. **Google:** Google's success can be attributed to its ability to identify and capitalize on emerging technology trends. By recognizing the potential of search engine technology and online advertising, Google became the dominant player in the digital advertising market.

9. **Tesla:** Tesla identified the demand for electric vehicles and sustainable

transportation solutions. By leveraging innovative technology and design, Tesla has positioned itself as a leader in the electric vehicle market, driving the transition towards renewable energy and environmentally-friendly transportation.

10. **Spotify:** Spotify identified the shift in consumer behavior towards digital music streaming. By offering a vast library of music content, personalized recommendations, and user-friendly features, Spotify has become the leading music streaming platform worldwide.

11. **Facebook:** Facebook identified the growing demand for social networking and online communication platforms. By providing a user-friendly interface, personalized content, and social networking features, Facebook revolutionized the way people connect and communicate online.

12. **Airbnb:** Airbnb identified the underutilization of spare rooms and properties as a business opportunity. By creating a platform that connects travelers with local hosts, Airbnb has disrupted the traditional hospitality industry and provided travelers with unique accommodation options.

13. **Slack:** Slack identified the need for efficient team communication and collaboration tools in the workplace. By offering a user-friendly interface, integrated features, and

customizable channels, Slack has become a popular choice for businesses seeking to streamline communication and enhance productivity.

14. **Zoom:** Zoom identified the demand for reliable and user-friendly video conferencing solutions. By offering high-quality video and audio, seamless screen sharing, and intuitive controls, Zoom has become a go-to platform for remote work, online meetings, and virtual events.

15. **Peloton:** Peloton identified the desire for convenient and engaging fitness experiences at home. By combining cutting-edge technology with immersive content and personalized coaching, Peloton has transformed the home fitness industry and attracted a dedicated community of users.

16. **Shopify:** Shopify identified the growing demand for e-commerce solutions among small and medium-sized businesses. By offering a user-friendly platform, customizable templates, and integrated tools, Shopify has empowered entrepreneurs to launch and scale online stores with ease.

17. **Trello:** Trello identified the need for visual project management tools that simplify task organization and collaboration. By offering a flexible and intuitive platform, Trello has become a popular choice for teams seeking to streamline workflow and improve productivity.

18. **Duolingo**: Duolingo identified the demand for accessible and engaging language learning tools. By offering gamified lessons, interactive exercises, and personalized feedback, Duolingo has made language learning fun and accessible to millions of users worldwide.

19. **Stripe:** Stripe identified the need for seamless online payment processing solutions for businesses. By offering a developer-friendly platform, flexible APIs, and robust security features, Stripe has become a leading provider of online payment infrastructure.

20. **Slack:** Slack identified the challenges of email overload and fragmented communication in the workplace. By offering a centralized messaging platform, integrated file sharing, and searchable archives, Slack has transformed the way teams communicate and collaborate.

21. **Coursera:** Coursera identified the demand for accessible and flexible online education. By partnering with top universities and offering a wide range of courses and specializations, Coursera has democratized access to quality education for learners around the world.

22. **Patreon:** Patreon identified the need for creators to monetize their content and connect with their audience. By offering a platform for creators to offer exclusive

content and receive ongoing support from fans, Patreon has empowered creators to earn a living doing what they love.

23. **Robinhood:** Robinhood identified the desire for accessible and commission-free trading platforms. By offering a user-friendly interface, instant trade execution, and no minimum account requirements, Robinhood has democratized access to the stock market for individual investors.

24. **Warby Parker:** Warby Parker identified the opportunity to disrupt the eyewear industry by offering affordable, stylish glasses online. By cutting out the middleman and offering a direct-to-consumer model, Warby Parker has gained a loyal customer base and transformed the way people buy glasses.

25. **Zappos:** Zappos identified the importance of customer service and satisfaction in e-commerce. By prioritizing customer experience and offering free shipping and returns, Zappos has built a reputation for exceptional service and earned the loyalty of millions of customers.

These case studies demonstrate the power of effective identification in driving innovation, disruption, and success in various industries. By understanding consumer needs, market trends, and emerging opportunities, organizations can position themselves for growth and create value for their customers and stakeholders.

Challenges and Limitations

Despite its importance, identification is not without its challenges and limitations. In some cases, individuals may struggle to accurately identify opportunities or challenges due to cognitive biases, blind spots, or limited perspective. Moreover, external factors such as market volatility, economic uncertainty, and competitive pressures can complicate the process of identification, making it difficult for individuals and organizations to anticipate changes and adapt effectively.

Furthermore, identification requires ongoing effort and vigilance to stay attuned to evolving trends, consumer preferences, and organizational dynamics. Without continuous monitoring and assessment, individuals and organizations may miss out on emerging opportunities or fail to address shifting challenges, jeopardizing their ability to achieve their goals.

It's critical to understand that identification serves as the cornerstone of achievement, guiding individuals and organizations towards success in personal and professional endeavors. By cultivating a keen sense of observation, proactive mindset, and strategic discernment, individuals and organizations can uncover hidden opportunities, confront challenges, and chart a course towards their goals. Whether in the realm of personal development or organizational success, effective identification is essential for driving growth, innovation, and positive change. As the first pillar of achievement, identification lays the groundwork for intentional action and sets the stage for transformative growth and accomplishment.

CHAPTER TWO

Pillar 2: Action - Bridging Vision and Reality

In the pursuit of any meaningful endeavor, the critical transition from contemplation to execution is marked by the second pillar of achievement: action. As the dynamic force that bridges the gap between envisioning a goal and transforming it into tangible reality, action propels individuals and organizations forward on their journey towards success. In this comprehensive exploration, we examine the critical nature of action, its role in driving progress, and the transformative impact it has on turning aspirations into achievements.

At its core, action embodies a proactive mindset and a commitment to taking decisive steps towards desired objectives. It is not merely about intention or planning but about putting plans into motion and making progress towards identified goals. Action requires individuals to move beyond the realm of contemplation and into the realm of execution, where ideas are transformed into concrete actions and results.

Moreover, action is characterized by a sense of urgency and momentum, driving individuals and organizations forward on their journey towards success. It involves setting priorities, allocating resources, and mobilizing efforts towards the achievement of defined objectives. By taking intentional and strategic action, individuals can create momentum that propels them closer to their goals, overcoming obstacles and setbacks along the way.

Furthermore, action is fueled by determination, perseverance, and resilience in the face of challenges and adversity. It requires individuals to confront obstacles head-on, adapt to changing circumstances, and persist in the pursuit of their goals. By embracing a mindset of resilience and perseverance, individuals can navigate the inevitable ups and downs of the achievement journey, staying focused and committed to their objectives.

Additionally, action fosters a sense of empowerment and agency, as individuals take control of their destiny and shape their own futures. By actively engaging in the pursuit of their goals, individuals gain a greater sense of autonomy and control over their lives, leading to increased confidence and self-efficacy. This empowerment fuels a positive feedback loop, as individuals draw inspiration and motivation from their progress, further propelling them towards success.

Action is the driving force that transforms aspirations into achievements, propelling individuals and organizations forward on their journey towards success. By embracing a proactive mindset, setting priorities, and persevering in the face of challenges, individuals can bridge the gap between vision and reality, turning their dreams into tangible outcomes. As the second pillar of achievement, action empowers individuals to take control of their destiny, realize their full potential, and create meaningful impact in their lives and communities.

Understanding Action

Action, as the second pillar of achievement, embodies more than the mere completion of tasks; it encapsulates a mindset of determination, perseverance, and strategic intent. It is the deliberate and intentional response to identified challenges or opportunities, characterized by careful planning, precise execution, and unwavering commitment. Whether at the individual level or within the context of an organization, action demands a proactive stance that converts aspirations into concrete results.

The Dynamics of Action

At its core, action is propelled by a sense of urgency and momentum, driving individuals and entities forward towards their goals. It involves breaking down complex objectives into manageable tasks, setting priorities, and taking decisive steps towards their realization. Moreover, action requires adaptability and resilience in the face of unforeseen obstacles or setbacks, as individuals navigate the twists and turns of the achievement journey.

Furthermore, action is fueled by a relentless pursuit of excellence and continuous improvement. It is not merely about achieving predefined outcomes but about striving for optimal performance and pushing the boundaries of possibility. By embracing a growth mindset and embracing feedback, individuals and organizations can refine their approach, learn from their experiences, and iterate towards greater success.

The Transformative Power of Action

Embracing action is essential for translating dreams into achievements and ideals into realities. It is the catalyst that propels individuals and entities from the realm of possibilities into the realm of actualization. By taking decisive steps towards their goals, individuals demonstrate their commitment to success and create momentum that propels them forward.

Moreover, action fosters a sense of empowerment and agency, as individuals take control of their destiny and shape their own futures. Rather than being passive spectators to the events unfolding around them, individuals who take action become active participants in the realization of their aspirations. This sense of agency instills a sense of purpose and fulfillment, as individuals witness the tangible impact of their efforts on their lives and the lives of others.

Practical Strategies for Effective Action

To harness the power of action effectively, individuals and organizations can adopt several strategies:

1. **Set clear goals:** Define specific, measurable, achievable, relevant, and time-bound (SMART) goals that provide a clear direction for action.
2. **Develop a plan:** Create a detailed action plan that outlines the steps needed to achieve your goals, including timelines, resources, and milestones.
3. **Prioritize tasks:** Identify the most critical tasks that will move you closer to your goals and focus your energy and resources on completing them.
4. **Stay adaptable:** Remain flexible and open to adjusting your approach as needed, based on changing circumstances or new information.
5. **Stay resilient:** Cultivate resilience and perseverance to overcome obstacles and setbacks, maintaining focus and momentum towards your goals.

By incorporating these strategies into their approach, individuals and organizations can harness the power of action to drive progress, achieve their goals, and realize their full potential.

Case Studies: Real-World Examples of Effective Action

To illustrate the transformative power of action, let us examine a few real-world examples:

1. **Mahatma Gandhi and the Indian Independence Movement**: Mahatma Gandhi's nonviolent resistance and civil disobedience tactics exemplify the power of action in driving social and political change. By mobilizing millions of people to take action against British colonial rule, Gandhi played a pivotal role in India's struggle for independence.

2. **Nelson Mandela and the Anti-Apartheid Movement**: Nelson Mandela's leadership and activism in the fight against apartheid in South Africa demonstrate the transformative impact of action. Through his unwavering commitment to justice and equality, Mandela inspired a generation to take action against institutionalized racism and oppression, leading to the eventual dismantling of apartheid.

3. **Rosa Parks and the Civil Rights Movement**: Rosa Parks' refusal to give up her seat on a segregated bus in Montgomery,

Alabama, sparked a wave of activism and protest that galvanized the Civil Rights Movement in the United States. By taking a bold stand against racial segregation, Parks ignited a movement that ultimately led to the end of Jim Crow laws and the advancement of civil rights for African Americans.

4. **Malala Yousafzai and Girls' Education**: Malala Yousafzai's advocacy for girls' education in Pakistan and around the world demonstrates the power of individual action in driving social change. Despite facing threats and violence from the Taliban, Malala continued to speak out for the rights of girls to receive an education, leading to increased awareness and support for girls' education globally.

5. **Bill and Melinda Gates Foundation:** The Bill and Melinda Gates Foundation's efforts to combat global poverty, improve healthcare, and advance education exemplify the transformative impact of philanthropic action. Through strategic investments in research, innovation, and public health initiatives, the foundation has made significant strides towards addressing some of the world's most pressing challenges.

6. **Greta Thunberg and Climate Activism:** Greta Thunberg's grassroots climate activism has sparked a global movement calling for urgent action to address climate change. By leading strikes, speaking at international

forums, and raising awareness about the climate crisis, Greta has inspired millions of young people to take action and demand meaningful change from world leaders.

7. **Doctors Without Borders:** Doctors Without Borders (Médecins Sans Frontières) provides medical care and humanitarian assistance to people in crisis zones around the world. By deploying medical teams to areas affected by conflict, natural disasters, and disease outbreaks, Doctors Without Borders demonstrates the lifesaving impact of direct action in response to humanitarian emergencies.

8. **Black Lives Matter Movement**: The Black Lives Matter movement mobilizes grassroots action to combat systemic racism and police violence against Black communities. Through protests, advocacy campaigns, and community organizing, activists have raised awareness about racial injustice and called for meaningful reforms to address systemic inequalities.

9. **The Suffragette Movement:** The Suffragette Movement fought for women's right to vote through direct action, protests, and civil disobedience. By organizing marches, hunger strikes, and acts of resistance, suffragettes brought attention to the issue of women's suffrage and ultimately secured the passage of the 19th Amendment

in the United States and similar reforms in other countries.

10. **The Civil Rights Act of 1964:** The Civil Rights Act of 1964 was a landmark piece of legislation that outlawed discrimination based on race, color, religion, sex, or national origin in the United States. Through grassroots organizing, advocacy, and nonviolent protests, civil rights activists pressured lawmakers to pass the legislation, leading to greater equality and justice for marginalized communities.

11. **The Occupy Wall Street Movement**: The Occupy Wall Street movement mobilized public action against economic inequality and corporate influence in politics. By organizing protests, sit-ins, and demonstrations, activists drew attention to the growing wealth gap and called for reforms to address the power imbalance between corporations and ordinary citizens.

12. **Marriage Equality Movement:** The marriage equality movement successfully campaigned for the legalization of same-sex marriage in countries around the world. Through grassroots organizing, legal advocacy, and public awareness campaigns, activists challenged discriminatory laws and societal attitudes, leading to landmark court rulings and legislative changes.

13. **The Arab Spring:** The Arab Spring was a series of protests and uprisings across the

Middle East and North Africa that called for political reform, democracy, and human rights. By organizing mass demonstrations, strikes, and civil disobedience, activists challenged authoritarian regimes and sparked political change in countries such as Tunisia, Egypt, and Libya.

14. **The #MeToo Movement:** The #MeToo movement mobilized action against sexual harassment and assault, empowering survivors to share their stories and hold perpetrators accountable. Through social media campaigns, advocacy efforts, and legal action, the movement raised awareness about the prevalence of sexual misconduct and called for systemic changes to address gender-based violence.

15. **The Environmental Justice Movement:** The environmental justice movement advocates for equitable access to clean air, water, and land for marginalized communities disproportionately affected by pollution and environmental degradation. Through grassroots organizing, community-led campaigns, and legal advocacy, activists work to address environmental racism and ensure that all people have the right to a healthy environment.

16. **The Global Fund to Fight AIDS, Tuberculosis, and Malaria**: The Global Fund is a partnership between governments, civil society, and the private sector that

mobilizes resources to combat HIV/AIDS, tuberculosis, and malaria worldwide. By providing funding for prevention, treatment, and care programs, the Global Fund has saved millions of lives and made significant progress towards ending these epidemics.

17. **The United Nations Sustainable Development Goals:** The United Nations Sustainable Development Goals (SDGs) provide a global framework for addressing pressing challenges such as poverty, inequality, and climate change. Through international cooperation, advocacy, and action at the local, national, and global levels, the SDGs aim to build a more sustainable and equitable future for all people and the planet.

18. **The Women's March:** The Women's March mobilizes action for women's rights, gender equality, and social justice through mass demonstrations, marches, and rallies. By bringing together diverse communities and amplifying women's voices, the Women's March advocates for policies and practices that advance gender equity and human rights.

19. **The Global Climate Strikes:** The Global Climate Strikes mobilize millions of people around the world to demand urgent action to address the climate crisis. By organizing strikes, rallies, and protests, climate activists call on governments and corporations to prioritize climate action, reduce greenhouse

gas emissions, and transition to renewable energy sources.

20. **The Youth-Led Movement for Gun Control:** The youth-led movement for gun control in the United States, exemplified by organizations such as March for Our Lives, mobilizes action to address gun violence and promote gun safety measures. By organizing protests, walkouts, and advocacy campaigns, young activists advocate for stricter gun laws and measures to prevent gun violence in schools and communities.

These case studies illustrate the power of effective action in driving social change, advancing human rights, and addressing pressing global challenges. Through grassroots organizing, advocacy, and direct action, individuals and communities can mobilize to create positive and lasting impact in their societies and around the world.

Challenges and Limitations

Despite its transformative potential, action is not without its challenges and limitations. In some cases, individuals may struggle to overcome inertia or fear of failure, preventing them from taking decisive steps towards their goals. Moreover, external factors such as resource constraints, institutional barriers, and systemic inequalities can impede the ability of individuals and organizations to take action effectively.

Furthermore, action requires careful planning and strategic execution to ensure that efforts are directed towards the most impactful outcomes. Without a clear understanding of priorities and objectives, individuals may find themselves expending energy and resources on tasks that do not contribute significantly to their goals. Additionally, action requires resilience and perseverance to overcome obstacles and setbacks along the way, as individuals navigate the inevitable challenges of the achievement journey.

Action is the driving force that propels individuals and organizations from vision to reality. By embracing a proactive mindset, strategic intent, and unwavering commitment, individuals can translate aspirations into achievements and ideals into realities. Whether in the realm of personal development, social change, or organizational success, action is essential for driving progress, realizing potential, and creating positive impact. As the second pillar of achievement, action empowers individuals to take control of their destiny, shape their own futures, and leave a lasting legacy of success.

CHAPTER THREE

Pillar 3: Education - Empowering Through Knowledge

With action set into motion, the third pillar, education, assumes a central role in the pursuit of achievement. Education, in this context, is not confined to formal institutions but encompasses a broader concept of continuous learning and knowledge acquisition. It is the process of equipping individuals and organizations with the tools and insights necessary to navigate the complexities inherent in their goals.

This pillar recognizes that informed decisions are potent decisions. Education empowers individuals by providing them with the understanding needed to navigate challenges, make informed choices, and innovate in the face of uncertainty. It involves learning from past experiences, staying abreast of industry trends, and embracing a mindset that thrives on curiosity and exploration.

Education serves as a guiding light, illuminating the path forward amidst ambiguity. It transforms individuals into lifelong learners, fostering adaptability and resilience. Whether through formal training programs, mentorship, or self-directed learning, this pillar ensures that the pursuit of achievement is underpinned by a robust foundation of knowledge.

Moreover, education serves as a catalyst for social change and economic development. By investing in education, societies can unlock the potential of their citizens, fostering innovation, entrepreneurship, and sustainable growth. Access to quality education empowers individuals from all backgrounds to overcome barriers, pursue their aspirations, and contribute meaningfully to their communities. In this way, education becomes a powerful tool for promoting social mobility and reducing inequality, creating a more equitable and inclusive society for all.

Furthermore, education plays a vital role in fostering global citizenship and promoting cross-cultural understanding. In an increasingly interconnected world, the ability to navigate cultural differences and communicate effectively across borders is essential for success. Education equips individuals with the knowledge, skills, and attitudes needed to engage with diverse perspectives and collaborate across cultural and geographical boundaries. By fostering empathy, tolerance, and respect for diversity, education lays the foundation for building a more peaceful and prosperous world.

Additionally, education empowers individuals to become lifelong learners, continuously seeking new knowledge and skills to adapt to evolving circumstances and seize opportunities for growth. In today's rapidly changing world, the pace of technological innovation and economic transformation requires individuals to embrace a mindset of lifelong learning and professional development. By staying curious, open-minded, and proactive in their pursuit of knowledge, individuals can remain relevant and resilient in the face of change, ensuring continued success and fulfillment in their personal and professional lives.

As individuals and organizations embark on their journey towards achievement, the critical role of education becomes evident. Serving as the third pillar of success, education plays a central role in empowering individuals and organizations through continuous learning and knowledge acquisition. In this comprehensive exploration, we examine the critical nature of education, its transformative impact on personal and professional development, and its crucial role in navigating the complexities inherent in the pursuit of achievement.

Education serves as a cornerstone of achievement, empowering individuals and organizations to realize their full potential and create positive change in the world. By fostering continuous learning, critical thinking, and global awareness, education equips individuals with the tools and insights needed to navigate challenges, seize opportunities, and make meaningful contributions to society. As the third pillar of achievement, education embodies the transformative power of knowledge, empowering individuals to thrive in an ever-changing world and build a brighter future for themselves and generations to come.

Understanding Education

Education, in the context of achievement, extends beyond the confines of formal institutions to encompass a broader concept of continuous learning and knowledge acquisition. It is the process of equipping individuals and organizations with the tools, insights, and skills necessary to navigate challenges, make informed decisions, and innovate in the face of uncertainty. Education serves as a catalyst for personal and professional growth, empowering individuals to realize their full potential and achieve their goals.

The Empowering Role of Education

At its core, education empowers individuals by providing them with the understanding and knowledge needed to navigate the complexities of their goals. Informed decisions are potent decisions, and education serves as the foundation upon which individuals can make informed choices that lead to success. By learning from past experiences, staying abreast of industry trends, and embracing a mindset of curiosity and exploration, individuals can continuously adapt and innovate in the pursuit of their objectives.

Moreover, education serves as a guiding light, illuminating the path forward amidst ambiguity and uncertainty. In a rapidly changing world, where new challenges and opportunities emerge constantly, the ability to learn and adapt is essential for success. Education transforms individuals into lifelong learners, fostering adaptability, resilience, and a growth mindset that enables them to thrive in dynamic and unpredictable environments.

Practical Applications of Education

Education can take many forms, ranging from formal training programs and academic degrees to mentorship, self-directed learning, and experiential learning opportunities. By engaging in continuous learning and knowledge acquisition, individuals can expand their skill set, deepen their understanding of their field, and stay ahead of the curve in an ever-evolving landscape. Moreover, education fosters creativity, innovation, and problem-solving skills, enabling individuals to approach challenges with confidence and ingenuity.

Furthermore, education promotes collaboration and knowledge sharing, as individuals exchange ideas, insights, and best practices with peers and colleagues. By participating in communities of practice, networking events, and professional development opportunities, individuals can leverage the collective wisdom of their peers to accelerate their learning and achieve their goals more effectively.

Case Studies: Real-World Examples of the Empowering Role of Education

To illustrate the transformative impact of education, let us examine a few real-world examples:

1. **Bill Gates:** Bill Gates, co-founder of Microsoft, is a renowned advocate for lifelong learning and continuous education. Despite dropping out of college, Gates pursued a self-directed education, voraciously reading books and attending seminars to deepen his understanding of computer programming and technology. This commitment to education laid the foundation for his success as a tech entrepreneur and philanthropist.

2. **Sheryl Sandberg:** Sheryl Sandberg, COO of Facebook, is a vocal proponent of mentorship and professional development. Throughout her career, Sandberg has sought out mentors and advisors who have helped her navigate challenges and seize opportunities. Moreover, Sandberg is an advocate for empowering women in the workplace,

leveraging her platform to promote initiatives that support gender equality and leadership development.

3. **Elon Musk:** Elon Musk, CEO of SpaceX and Tesla, is known for his relentless pursuit of knowledge and innovation. Musk has a diverse educational background, having studied physics, economics, and engineering at various institutions. Moreover, Musk is a voracious reader and lifelong learner, constantly seeking to expand his knowledge and understanding of the world. This commitment to education has enabled Musk to push the boundaries of technology and drive progress in industries ranging from space exploration to electric vehicles.

4. **Malala Yousafzai**: Malala Yousafzai, a Pakistani activist for female education, became a global symbol of the fight for girls' education after surviving an assassination attempt by the Taliban in 2012. Despite facing threats and violence, Malala continued to advocate for girls' right to education, eventually becoming the youngest-ever Nobel Prize laureate in 2014. Her courage and resilience have inspired millions around the world to prioritize education and empower girls to pursue their dreams.

5. **Jamie Oliver**: Celebrity chef Jamie Oliver is known not only for his culinary skills but also for his efforts to promote food education and improve nutrition in schools. Through

initiatives like his Food Revolution campaign, Oliver has advocated for healthier school meals and comprehensive food education programs to empower children and families to make healthier choices. His work has led to significant policy changes and improvements in school food environments around the world.

6. **Michelle Obama**: Former First Lady Michelle Obama has been a vocal advocate for education and empowerment, particularly for girls and women. Through initiatives like the Let Girls Learn program, Obama has worked to expand access to education for girls around the world, recognizing the transformative impact that education can have on individuals, families, and communities. Her advocacy has helped raise awareness of the importance of education and inspired action to support girls' education globally.

7. **Sal Khan**: Sal Khan is the founder of Khan Academy, a non-profit organization that provides free, world-class education to anyone, anywhere. Khan's vision is to democratize access to education and empower learners of all ages to unlock their full potential through personalized, self-paced learning. Khan Academy has become a global leader in online education, reaching millions of learners around the world and

empowering them to achieve their academic goals.

8. **Malcom X:** Civil rights activist Malcom X exemplified the transformative power of education in his own life. While serving a prison sentence, Malcom X educated himself by reading voraciously and studying a wide range of subjects. His self-directed education transformed him from a troubled youth into one of the most influential leaders of the civil rights movement. Malcom X's journey underscores the importance of education in empowering individuals to overcome adversity and effect meaningful change.

9. **Oprah Winfrey:** Media mogul Oprah Winfrey overcame a challenging childhood marked by poverty and abuse through the power of education. Despite facing numerous obstacles, Winfrey pursued her education relentlessly, eventually earning a scholarship to college and launching a successful career in media. Throughout her career, Winfrey has emphasized the importance of lifelong learning and personal development, inspiring millions to pursue their educational aspirations and achieve their goals.

10. **Sundar Pichai:** CEO of Google, Sundar Pichai, is a prime example of the transformative impact of education. Born in India, Pichai earned a scholarship to study at Stanford University, where he completed a master's degree in engineering and later

earned an MBA from the Wharton School of the University of Pennsylvania. Pichai's educational background equipped him with the skills and knowledge needed to succeed in the tech industry, eventually leading him to become one of the most influential leaders in the world.

11. **Nelson Mandela:** Nelson Mandela, former President of South Africa, recognized the power of education to transform individuals and societies. While imprisoned for 27 years, Mandela continued his education by studying law and politics through correspondence courses. Upon his release, Mandela became a leading advocate for education and worked to expand access to education for all South Africans, particularly those who had been marginalized under apartheid. Mandela's commitment to education helped lay the foundation for a more inclusive and equitable society in South Africa.

12. **Oprah Winfrey:** Media mogul Oprah Winfrey overcame a challenging childhood marked by poverty and abuse through the power of education. Despite facing numerous obstacles, Winfrey pursued her education relentlessly, eventually earning a scholarship to college and launching a successful career in media. Throughout her career, Winfrey has emphasized the importance of lifelong learning and personal development, inspiring

millions to pursue their educational aspirations and achieve their goals.

13. **Elon Musk:** Entrepreneur Elon Musk, CEO of SpaceX and Tesla, embodies the transformative impact of education on innovation and progress. Musk's insatiable curiosity and commitment to learning have driven him to master multiple disciplines, from engineering and physics to business and technology. His educational background has equipped him with the knowledge and skills needed to revolutionize industries ranging from space exploration to electric vehicles, demonstrating the power of education to fuel innovation and drive positive change.

14. **Angela Merkel:** Angela Merkel, Chancellor of Germany, is a trained physicist who leveraged her educational background to become one of the world's most influential political leaders. Merkel's scientific training instilled in her a rigorous analytical mindset and a commitment to evidence-based decision-making, qualities that have served her well in navigating complex political challenges. Merkel's educational background highlights the importance of interdisciplinary learning and critical thinking in leadership roles.

15. **Lin-Manuel Miranda:** Playwright and composer Lin-Manuel Miranda used his education to create groundbreaking works of art that have had a profound impact on culture

and society. Miranda's musical "Hamilton," which explores the life of Founding Father Alexander Hamilton, has been hailed as a cultural phenomenon and has won numerous awards, including the Pulitzer Prize for Drama. Miranda's education in history and theater provided him with the knowledge and inspiration to create innovative and influential works of art.

16. **Marie Curie:** Physicist and chemist Marie Curie made groundbreaking discoveries in the field of radioactivity, earning her two Nobel Prizes in Physics and Chemistry. Curie's education in science and mathematics provided her with the foundation needed to conduct pioneering research that revolutionized our understanding of the physical world. Her achievements serve as a testament to the transformative power of education in unlocking human potential and advancing knowledge.

17. **Wangari Maathai:** Environmentalist Wangari Maathai was the founder of the Green Belt Movement, an organization that empowered women in Kenya to plant trees and combat deforestation. Maathai's education in biology and environmental science equipped her with the knowledge and skills needed to address pressing environmental issues and mobilize grassroots action. Her work earned her the Nobel Peace Prize in 2004 and inspired a global movement

for environmental conservation and social justice.

18. **Steve Jobs:** Entrepreneur Steve Jobs, co-founder of Apple Inc., revolutionized the technology industry through his innovative products and visionary leadership. Jobs' education in design and technology provided him with the foundation needed to create iconic products like the iPhone, iPad, and MacBook. His commitment to excellence and his passion for education continue to inspire millions of aspiring entrepreneurs and innovators around the world.

19. **Serena Williams:** Tennis champion Serena Williams used her education to become one of the greatest athletes of all time. Despite facing racial and gender barriers in the sport, Williams pursued her education in tennis from a young age, honing her skills through practice and perseverance. Her dedication to her craft and her commitment to continuous improvement have made her a role model for aspiring athletes and a symbol of empowerment for women and girls everywhere.

20. **Warren Buffett:** Investor Warren Buffett, CEO of Berkshire Hathaway, is known for his disciplined approach to investing and his commitment to lifelong learning. Buffett credits much of his success to his voracious reading habits and his insatiable curiosity about the world. His educational background

in finance and his deep understanding of business fundamentals have made him one of the most successful investors of all time, demonstrating the transformative power of education in the world of finance and investing.

21. **Mary Jackson:** Mary Jackson was an aerospace engineer and mathematician who broke barriers as the first African American female engineer at NASA. Jackson's education in mathematics and engineering provided her with the foundation needed to excel in a male-dominated field and contribute to groundbreaking projects like the Apollo program. Her achievements paved the way for future generations of women and minorities in STEM fields, demonstrating the transformative impact of education on diversity and inclusion.

22. **Greta Thunberg:** Environmental activist Greta Thunberg used her education to raise awareness about climate change and advocate for urgent action to address the climate crisis. Despite being just a teenager, Thunberg's knowledge of climate science and her passion for environmental activism have inspired millions of young people around the world to join the fight for climate justice. Her education has empowered her to speak truth to power and hold world leaders accountable for their actions on climate change.

23. **Nelson Mandela:** Nelson Mandela, former President of South Africa, recognized the power of education to transform individuals and societies. While imprisoned for 27 years, Mandela continued his education by studying law and politics through correspondence courses. Upon his release, Mandela became a leading advocate for education and worked to expand access to education for all South Africans, particularly those who had been marginalized under apartheid. Mandela's commitment to education helped lay the foundation for a more inclusive and equitable society in South Africa.

These examples highlight the transformative power of education in empowering individuals to achieve their goals and make a positive impact in the world. By embracing a mindset of continuous learning and knowledge acquisition, individuals can unlock their full potential and create opportunities for success and fulfillment.

Challenges and Opportunities in Education

Despite its transformative potential, education is not without its challenges and opportunities. In some cases, individuals may face barriers to accessing quality education, such as financial constraints, geographic limitations, or systemic inequalities. Moreover, the rapid pace of technological change and globalization presents new challenges and opportunities for education, requiring individuals to adapt and evolve in order to stay relevant in an increasingly competitive and interconnected world.

Furthermore, traditional models of education may not always align with the needs of a rapidly changing workforce, requiring individuals to seek out alternative pathways to learning and skill development. Moreover, the rise of online learning platforms, Massive Open Online Courses (MOOCs), and other digital learning resources presents new opportunities for individuals to access high-quality education and training from anywhere in the world.

Education serves as a cornerstone of achievement, empowering individuals and organizations through continuous learning and knowledge acquisition. By embracing a mindset of lifelong learning, individuals can expand their skill set, deepen their understanding of their field, and stay ahead of the curve in an ever-evolving landscape. Moreover, education fosters creativity, innovation, and problem-solving skills, enabling individuals to approach challenges with confidence and ingenuity. As the third pillar of achievement, education provides individuals with the tools, insights, and skills necessary to navigate challenges, make informed decisions, and innovate in the pursuit of their goals. By embracing a commitment to continuous learning and knowledge acquisition, individuals can unlock their full potential and achieve success and fulfillment in their personal and professional lives.

CHAPTER FOUR

Pillar 4: Application - Transforming Knowledge into Action

Armed with knowledge, the fourth pillar, application, takes center stage in the journey toward achievement. It involves the practical implementation of the insights acquired through the education phase. Application is the bridge that connects theory to practice, transforming abstract knowledge into tangible results.

This pillar requires a willingness to experiment, take calculated risks, and adapt to changing circumstances. It's not enough to possess knowledge; the true measure of success lies in the ability to apply that knowledge effectively. Whether in personal development or organizational strategy, the application is where ideas gain traction and evolve into impactful outcomes.

Embracing the application phase involves a shift from passive learning to active engagement. It requires individuals and entities to assess their environment, identify opportunities for implementation, and execute with precision. This dynamic interplay between knowledge and action propels the achievement journey forward, bringing about tangible progress and real-world impact.

As individuals and organizations strive for success, armed with knowledge acquired through education, the crucial transition to the fourth pillar, application, becomes paramount. Application is the practical implementation of insights gained from the education phase, serving as the bridge between theory and practice. In this comprehensive exploration, we examine the critical nature of application, its role in driving tangible results, and its transformative impact on the journey towards achievement.

Furthermore, the process of application demands a strategic approach that goes beyond mere execution. It requires individuals and organizations to develop clear objectives, establish measurable goals, and devise actionable plans to achieve desired outcomes. This strategic mindset ensures that the application of knowledge is purposeful and aligned with overarching objectives, maximizing the likelihood of success.

Moreover, effective application often involves collaboration and teamwork, as individuals pool their knowledge and resources to tackle complex challenges and achieve common goals. By leveraging diverse perspectives and expertise, teams can generate innovative solutions and overcome obstacles that may be insurmountable for individuals working alone. Collaboration fosters synergy and creativity, leading to more robust and sustainable outcomes in the pursuit of achievement.

Additionally, the process of application is iterative, requiring continuous evaluation and refinement to optimize results over time. Through ongoing monitoring and feedback, individuals and organizations can identify areas for improvement, make necessary adjustments, and adapt their approaches in response to changing circumstances. This iterative approach fosters a culture of continuous learning and improvement, ensuring that the application of knowledge remains dynamic and responsive to evolving needs and opportunities.

Furthermore, effective application requires a willingness to embrace failure and learn from setbacks along the way. Not every idea will yield the desired results on the first try, and setbacks are inevitable in any journey toward achievement. However, by viewing failure as an opportunity for growth rather than a roadblock to success, individuals can extract valuable lessons, refine their approaches, and ultimately achieve greater success in the long run.

The fourth pillar of achievement, application, is the linchpin that transforms knowledge into action and drives tangible results. It requires a strategic mindset, collaboration, iteration, and a willingness to learn from failure. By effectively applying knowledge in personal development and organizational strategy, individuals and organizations can turn ideas into impactful outcomes, driving progress and success in their respective endeavors.

Understanding Application

Application involves translating theoretical knowledge into practical action, leveraging insights gained through education to bring about real-world outcomes. It requires a proactive approach, where individuals and entities take deliberate steps to apply their knowledge in relevant contexts. This pillar emphasizes the importance of action-oriented thinking and the willingness to experiment, take risks, and adapt to changing circumstances in pursuit of goals.

The Role of Application in Achievement

At its core, application is where ideas come to life and evolve into impactful outcomes. It represents the culmination of the learning process, where knowledge is transformed into tangible results that drive progress and create value. Whether in personal development or organizational strategy, the ability to apply knowledge effectively is essential for achieving success. It is not enough to possess knowledge; success hinges on the ability to translate that knowledge into action and produce meaningful results.

Moreover, embracing the application phase involves a shift from passive learning to active engagement. It requires individuals and entities to assess their environment, identify opportunities for implementation, and execute with precision. By taking proactive steps to apply their knowledge, individuals can unlock their full potential and maximize their impact in their personal and professional lives.

Practical Applications of Application

Application can take many forms, ranging from implementing new strategies and initiatives to solving complex problems and seizing opportunities. For individuals, application may involve applying newly acquired skills and knowledge to advance their careers or achieve personal goals. For organizations, application may entail implementing innovative solutions to address challenges or capitalize on emerging trends in the market.

Furthermore, application requires a willingness to take calculated risks and embrace uncertainty. It involves stepping outside of one's comfort zone, experimenting with new ideas, and learning from both successes and failures. By taking calculated risks and adapting to changing circumstances, individuals and entities can iterate and improve their approaches, ultimately driving greater success and innovation.

Case Studies: Real-World Examples of Effective Application

To illustrate the transformative impact of application, let us examine a few real-world examples:

1. **Airbnb:** Airbnb is a prime example of effective application, transforming the hospitality industry through its innovative platform that connects travelers with local hosts. By applying technology and leveraging the sharing economy model, Airbnb has disrupted traditional hotel chains and provided millions of travelers with unique and affordable accommodation options around the world.

2. **SpaceX:** SpaceX, founded by entrepreneur Elon Musk, exemplifies effective application in the aerospace industry. By applying cutting-edge technology and innovative engineering solutions, SpaceX has revolutionized space travel and reduced the cost of launching payloads into orbit. Through successful missions to the International Space Station and ambitious plans for Mars colonization, SpaceX has demonstrated the power of application to push the boundaries of what is possible in space exploration.

3. **Apple Inc.:** Apple Inc. is renowned for its innovative products and design-driven approach to technology. By applying insights from user experience research and human-centered design principles, Apple has created iconic products like the iPhone, iPad, and MacBook that resonate with consumers worldwide. Through meticulous attention to detail and a commitment to quality, Apple has set the standard for excellence in product design and customer experience.

4. **Google:** Google is a global leader in technology and innovation, known for its groundbreaking search engine and diverse portfolio of products and services. By applying advanced algorithms and machine learning techniques, Google has revolutionized the way we access and organize information online. From search to artificial intelligence, Google continues to push the boundaries of innovation through its relentless pursuit of new ideas and technologies.

5. **Mahatma Gandhi**: Mahatma Gandhi, the leader of India's independence movement, exemplifies effective application in the realm of social change. Through nonviolent resistance and civil disobedience, Gandhi led India to independence from British colonial rule, inspiring similar movements for justice and equality around the world. By applying the principles of truth, nonviolence, and

compassion, Gandhi demonstrated the transformative power of application in effecting positive change on a global scale.

6. **Amazon:** Amazon's application of data analytics and machine learning algorithms has transformed the e-commerce industry. By leveraging customer data to personalize recommendations and optimize logistics, Amazon has revolutionized the online shopping experience, driving significant growth and customer loyalty.

7. **Toyota Production System**: Toyota's application of lean manufacturing principles has led to greater efficiency, quality, and innovation in automobile production. By implementing practices such as just-in-time inventory management and continuous improvement, Toyota has become a global leader in automotive manufacturing, setting the standard for excellence in lean production.

8. **IBM Watson**: IBM's application of artificial intelligence through its Watson platform has enabled breakthroughs in healthcare, finance, and other industries. By analyzing vast amounts of data and generating actionable insights, Watson has helped healthcare providers improve diagnoses, financial institutions detect fraud, and businesses make smarter decisions.

9. **Patagonia:** Patagonia's application of sustainable business practices has set a new

standard for corporate environmental responsibility. By prioritizing environmental conservation and social responsibility in its operations, Patagonia has demonstrated that businesses can thrive while also making a positive impact on the planet.

10. **The Gates Foundation:** The Gates Foundation's application of philanthropic resources has catalyzed progress in global health and development. By investing in initiatives such as vaccine research, disease eradication, and education reform, the Gates Foundation has helped save millions of lives and improve the well-being of people around the world.

11. **Tesla:** Tesla's application of electric vehicle technology has accelerated the transition to sustainable transportation. By designing and manufacturing high-performance electric cars, Tesla has challenged the dominance of traditional automakers and paved the way for a future of clean, renewable energy.

12. **Duolingo:** Duolingo's application of gamification principles has made language learning fun, accessible, and effective for millions of users worldwide. By turning language learning into a game-like experience, Duolingo has engaged learners of all ages and skill levels, helping them achieve fluency in new languages.

13. **Starbucks:** Starbucks' application of customer-centric strategies has fueled its

growth and success in the competitive coffee industry. By prioritizing customer experience and innovation, Starbucks has built a loyal customer base and established itself as a global leader in specialty coffee.

14. **Wikipedia:** Wikipedia's application of collaborative editing has democratized access to knowledge and created the world's largest encyclopedia. By allowing anyone to contribute and edit articles, Wikipedia has enabled the free exchange of information and empowered individuals to share their expertise with the world.

15. **Netflix:** Netflix's application of data-driven algorithms has revolutionized the entertainment industry and transformed how people consume media. By analyzing user preferences and viewing habits, Netflix can recommend personalized content to its subscribers, leading to increased engagement and customer satisfaction.

16. **Slack:** Slack's application of team communication software has streamlined collaboration and productivity in the workplace. By providing a centralized platform for messaging, file sharing, and project management, Slack has reduced email overload and improved communication efficiency for teams around the world.

17. **Zoom:** Zoom's application of video conferencing technology has transformed remote work and virtual communication. By

offering high-quality video and audio capabilities, Zoom has enabled teams to collaborate effectively from anywhere, leading to increased productivity and flexibility in the modern workplace.

18. **Coursera:** Coursera's application of online education technology has democratized access to higher education and lifelong learning. By partnering with top universities and institutions to offer online courses and degrees, Coursera has expanded access to quality education for millions of learners worldwide.

19. **23andMe:** 23andMe's application of genetic testing technology has revolutionized personalized healthcare and genetic research. By offering direct-to-consumer DNA testing kits, 23andMe has empowered individuals to learn about their genetic ancestry, health risks, and predispositions, leading to greater awareness and informed decision-making about health and wellness.

20. **Khan Academy:** Khan Academy's application of online learning technologies has democratized access to education and empowered millions of learners worldwide. By providing free, high-quality educational resources in subjects ranging from math to art history, Khan Academy has leveled the playing field for students of all backgrounds and abilities.

Challenges and Opportunities in Application

Despite its transformative potential, application is not without its challenges and opportunities. In some cases, individuals and organizations may struggle to translate knowledge into action due to various barriers, such as resource constraints, institutional inertia, or resistance to change. Moreover, the fast-paced nature of the modern world presents new challenges and opportunities for application, requiring individuals and entities to adapt quickly and innovate in order to stay ahead of the curve.

Furthermore, effective application requires a supportive ecosystem that fosters collaboration, creativity, and risk-taking. By creating an environment where individuals feel empowered to experiment, iterate, and learn from their experiences, organizations can unleash the full potential of their people and drive greater innovation and success. Moreover, investing in education and training programs can help individuals develop the skills and competencies needed to apply their knowledge effectively and achieve their goals.

Application serves as the transformative engine that drives progress and creates value in the journey towards achievement. By translating knowledge into action, individuals and organizations can turn ideas into reality, solve complex problems, and seize opportunities for growth and innovation. As the fourth pillar of achievement, application embodies the power of proactive

CHAPTER FIVE

Pillar 5: Appreciation - Cultivating Recognition and Acknowledgment

As the journey unfolds, the fifth pillar, appreciation, comes to the forefront. It is the recognition and acknowledgment of efforts and achievements throughout the process. This pillar underscores the importance of fostering a positive and supportive environment, cultivating motivation, and reinforcing the value of collaborative endeavors.

Appreciation extends beyond celebrating the end results; it encompasses acknowledging the incremental victories, improvements, and contributions of individuals involved in the pursuit of success. This recognition serves as a powerful motivator, nurturing a sense of purpose and commitment among those engaged in the achievement journey.

Within organizations, a culture of appreciation contributes to employee satisfaction, engagement, and retention. On an individual level, self-appreciation becomes a driving force for continued personal development. The fifth pillar, appreciation, thus plays a pivotal role in sustaining momentum, fostering a sense of camaraderie, and creating an environment where achievements are celebrated at every step.

As individuals and organizations embark on their journey towards achievement, the critical role of appreciation becomes evident. Serving as the fifth pillar of success, appreciation is the recognition and acknowledgment of efforts and achievements throughout the process. In this comprehensive exploration, we examine the critical nature of appreciation, its transformative impact on motivation and morale, and its crucial role in cultivating a positive and supportive environment conducive to success.

In addition to acknowledging individual efforts, appreciation also serves to strengthen the bonds within teams and organizations. When individuals feel valued and appreciated for their contributions, it fosters a sense of camaraderie and mutual respect among team members. This, in turn, leads to greater collaboration, communication, and cohesion within the group, ultimately enhancing overall productivity and performance.

Moreover, appreciation acts as a morale booster, particularly during challenging times or periods of uncertainty. By recognizing and celebrating even the smallest victories and contributions, leaders can uplift the spirits of their team members and instill a sense of optimism and resilience. This positivity can help mitigate stress, boost morale, and inspire individuals to persevere in the face of adversity.

Furthermore, appreciation promotes a culture of gratitude and kindness within organizations, leading to greater job satisfaction and employee engagement. When employees feel appreciated for their hard work and dedication, they are more likely to feel fulfilled and motivated in their roles. This, in turn, can lead to higher levels of job satisfaction, lower turnover rates, and increased loyalty to the organization. Appreciation serves as a powerful tool for employee recognition and retention. When employees feel valued and appreciated, they are more likely to remain committed to their organization and go above and beyond in their roles. This can help reduce turnover costs and improve employee retention rates, ultimately contributing to the long-term success and stability of the organization.

Appreciation is a fundamental pillar of achievement that fosters a positive and supportive environment, cultivates motivation, and reinforces the value of collaborative endeavors. By acknowledging the efforts and contributions of individuals, teams, and organizations, appreciation serves as a powerful motivator, morale booster, and driver of success. As leaders and organizations continue on their journey towards achievement, embracing and practicing appreciation will be essential in fostering a culture of positivity, gratitude, and growth.

Understanding Appreciation

Appreciation goes beyond mere acknowledgment of end results; it encompasses recognizing the incremental victories, improvements, and contributions of individuals involved in the pursuit of success. This pillar underscores the importance of fostering a culture of recognition and acknowledgment, where efforts are celebrated, and achievements are valued at every step of the journey. By expressing gratitude and appreciation, individuals and organizations can cultivate motivation, reinforce positive behavior, and foster a sense of belonging and camaraderie among team members.

The Role of Appreciation in Achievement

At its core, appreciation serves as a powerful motivator, nurturing a sense of purpose and commitment among those engaged in the achievement journey. By acknowledging the efforts and contributions of individuals, appreciation fosters a positive feedback loop, where recognition fuels motivation and drives continued success. Within organizations, a culture of appreciation contributes to employee satisfaction, engagement, and retention, ultimately leading to higher productivity and performance.

Moreover, appreciation plays a pivotal role in sustaining momentum and morale during challenging times. By celebrating even the smallest victories and milestones, individuals and organizations can maintain a positive outlook and overcome obstacles with resilience and determination. In times of adversity, expressions of appreciation serve as a beacon of encouragement, reminding individuals of their value and contribution to the collective effort.

Practical Applications of Appreciation

Appreciation can take many forms, ranging from verbal praise and recognition to tangible rewards and incentives. Within organizations, leaders can foster a culture of appreciation by regularly acknowledging the efforts and achievements of their team members through verbal recognition, performance bonuses, employee of the month awards, and other forms of appreciation. Additionally, team-building activities, such as group outings or team lunches, can provide opportunities for colleagues to express gratitude and appreciation for each other's contributions in a more informal setting.

Furthermore, appreciation extends beyond the workplace to encompass personal relationships and community involvement. In family settings, expressing gratitude and appreciation for each other's support and contributions can strengthen bonds and foster a sense of harmony and unity. Similarly, in community settings, acknowledging the efforts of volunteers and community members can inspire others to get involved and make a positive impact in their own neighborhoods and beyond.

Case Studies: Real-World Examples of Effective Appreciation

To illustrate the transformative impact of appreciation, let us examine a few real-world examples:

1. **Google:** Google is known for its innovative approach to employee appreciation, offering perks such as free gourmet meals, on-site fitness centers, and massage therapy services. Additionally, Google has a peer recognition program where employees can nominate their colleagues for "spot awards" to recognize their outstanding contributions to the company.

2. **Southwest Airlines**: Southwest Airlines has a unique culture of appreciation known as "LUV," which stands for "Living the Southwest Way." Employees are encouraged to recognize and celebrate each other's achievements through a variety of channels, including company-wide meetings, social media shoutouts, and handwritten notes from leadership.

3. **Charity: Water: Charity:** Water, a nonprofit organization dedicated to providing clean and safe drinking water to people in developing countries, places a strong emphasis on donor appreciation. The organization regularly sends personalized thank-you notes and updates to its donors, recognizing their generosity and the impact of their contributions on the lives of others.

4. **Google's Peer Bonus Program**: Google encourages appreciation among its employees through its Peer Bonus Program, where employees can nominate their colleagues for exceptional contributions. This program allows employees to recognize and reward each other's efforts, fostering a culture of appreciation and teamwork within the organization.

5. **Southwest Airlines' "Spirit of Appreciation" Program:** Southwest Airlines values appreciation as a core part of its company culture. The airline has a program called "Spirit of Appreciation," where employees can nominate their peers for going above and beyond in their roles. This program helps reinforce the company's values and encourages employees to recognize and celebrate each other's achievements.

6. **Zappos' "Zollar" Recognition System:** At Zappos, the online shoe and clothing retailer, employees use a currency called "Zollars" to

recognize and appreciate each other's contributions. Zollars can be earned through various acts of kindness, teamwork, and exceptional performance. Employees can then redeem their Zollars for rewards, creating a culture of appreciation and recognition within the company.

7. **Microsoft's "Thank You" Platform:** Microsoft has a platform called "Thank You" where employees can publicly recognize and appreciate their colleagues for their hard work and contributions. This platform allows employees to express their gratitude and appreciation in a visible and meaningful way, fostering a positive work environment and sense of camaraderie within the organization.

8. **Patagonia's Employee Appreciation Days:** Patagonia, the outdoor clothing and gear company, holds regular Employee Appreciation Days to recognize and celebrate the hard work and dedication of its employees. These events often include activities, awards ceremonies, and special perks for employees, reinforcing the company's commitment to appreciation and employee well-being.

9. **Pixar's "Peer Recognition" Program:** Pixar Animation Studios encourages appreciation among its employees through its "Peer Recognition" program. Employees can nominate their colleagues for recognition based on their contributions to projects,

teamwork, and creative excellence. This program helps foster a culture of appreciation and collaboration within the studio.

10. **Cisco's "You Earned It" Recognition Program**: Cisco, the multinational technology conglomerate, has a recognition program called "You Earned It" where employees can give and receive recognition for their achievements and contributions. This program allows employees to express their appreciation for each other's hard work and dedication, contributing to a positive work environment and employee engagement.

11. **Hilton's "Catch Me at My Best" Program:** Hilton Hotels & Resorts encourages appreciation among its employees through its "Catch Me at My Best" program. Employees can nominate their colleagues for recognition based on exemplary performance and acts of kindness. This program helps reinforce Hilton's commitment to customer service and employee recognition.

12. **LinkedIn's "InDay" Program:** LinkedIn, the professional networking platform, has a program called "InDay" where employees can take a day off to volunteer or pursue personal projects. This program demonstrates LinkedIn's appreciation for its employees' hard work and dedication by giving them time to recharge and pursue their passions outside of work.

13. **Starbucks' "Partner of the Quarter" Awards:** Starbucks recognizes and appreciates its employees through its "Partner of the Quarter" awards. Employees can nominate their colleagues for recognition based on outstanding performance, customer service, and teamwork. This program helps reinforce Starbucks' commitment to employee appreciation and recognition.

14. **Adobe's "You Rock" Recognition Program:** Adobe, the software company, has a recognition program called "You Rock" where employees can give and receive recognition for their contributions and achievements. This program allows employees to express their appreciation for each other's hard work and dedication, fostering a positive work environment and sense of camaraderie.

15. **The Ritz-Carlton's "Employee of the Month" Program:** The Ritz-Carlton hotels recognize and appreciate their employees through their "Employee of the Month" program. Employees can nominate their colleagues for recognition based on exceptional service, teamwork, and dedication to guest satisfaction. This program helps reinforce The Ritz-Carlton's commitment to excellence in hospitality and employee recognition.

16. **Airbnb's "Superhost" Program:** Airbnb recognizes and appreciates its top-

performing hosts through its "Superhost" program. Hosts who consistently provide exceptional hospitality and receive positive reviews from guests are awarded the "Superhost" designation, along with special perks and recognition from Airbnb. This program helps incentivize hosts to deliver outstanding experiences and fosters a sense of appreciation within the Airbnb host community.

17. **Whole Foods' "Team Member Appreciation Week":** Whole Foods Market holds an annual "Team Member Appreciation Week" to recognize and celebrate the hard work and dedication of its employees. During this week, employees receive special discounts, perks, and recognition for their contributions to the company. This event helps foster a positive work environment and reinforces Whole Foods' commitment to employee appreciation.

18. **REI's "Peak Awards":** REI, the outdoor retail co-op, recognizes and appreciates its employees through its "Peak Awards" program. Employees can nominate their colleagues for recognition based on exceptional performance, customer service, and contributions to the company's mission. This program helps reinforce REI's values of stewardship, authenticity, and respect for the outdoors.

Challenges and Opportunities in Cultivating Appreciation

Despite its many benefits, cultivating a culture of appreciation can present challenges, particularly in large organizations or in environments where recognition is not prioritized. Additionally, ensuring that appreciation is genuine and meaningful requires a nuanced understanding of individual preferences and motivations. Moreover, in diverse and multicultural settings, it is essential to recognize and respect cultural differences in expressions of appreciation, ensuring that all individuals feel valued and respected.

Furthermore, the fast-paced nature of modern life can make it easy to overlook the importance of appreciation in the pursuit of success. In a world where instant gratification and tangible outcomes are often prioritized, the intangible benefits of appreciation may be undervalued or overlooked. However, by taking the time to express gratitude and acknowledge the efforts of others, individuals and organizations can cultivate a culture of appreciation that fosters mutual respect, trust, and collaboration.

Appreciation serves as a cornerstone of achievement, fostering recognition and acknowledgment of efforts and achievements throughout the journey towards success. By cultivating a culture of appreciation, individuals and organizations can nurture motivation, morale, and collaboration, ultimately driving greater productivity, satisfaction, and success. As the fifth pillar of achievement, appreciation embodies the power of gratitude and recognition in creating positive change and fostering a sense of belonging and purpose in the pursuit of shared goals and aspirations.

CHAPTER SIX

Pillar 6: Compensation - Recognizing and Rewarding Contributions

In the realm of achievement, the sixth pillar, compensation, acknowledges the intrinsic link between effort and reward. Compensation goes beyond monetary rewards; it encompasses various forms of recognition and acknowledgment for the contributions of individuals. This pillar underscores the importance of fairness, equity, and the establishment of a symbiotic relationship between achievement and recognition.

Compensation serves as a powerful motivator, incentivizing individuals and teams to consistently strive for excellence. It recognizes the value of dedication, innovation, and sustained effort, fostering a culture where contributions are not only acknowledged but also appropriately rewarded. Whether through promotions, bonuses, or non-monetary gestures, compensation reinforces the reciprocal nature of the achievement journey.

On an organizational level, effective compensation strategies contribute to employee satisfaction, loyalty, and a positive work culture. It aligns individual goals with organizational objectives, creating a harmonious synergy that propels the entire entity toward greater success. The sixth pillar, compensation, thus becomes a key element in sustaining a thriving ecosystem of achievement.

In the realm of achievement, the importance of recognizing and rewarding contributions cannot be overstated. Compensation, as the sixth pillar of success, serves as a pivotal element in acknowledging the intrinsic link between effort and reward. While often associated with monetary remuneration, compensation encompasses a broader spectrum of recognition and acknowledgment for individual contributions. This comprehensive exploration examine the critical nature of compensation, its significance in fostering motivation and engagement, and its role in establishing a culture of fairness and equity within organizations.

Compensation, as the sixth pillar of achievement, plays a pivotal role in fostering a culture where effort is recognized and rewarded. Beyond simply providing monetary compensation, effective recognition encompasses various forms of acknowledgment, including promotions, bonuses, and non-monetary gestures. This holistic approach emphasizes the intrinsic link between individual contributions and organizational success, reinforcing the symbiotic relationship between achievement and recognition.

Fairness and equity are fundamental principles underlying effective compensation strategies.

Employees value transparency and consistency in how rewards are allocated, ensuring that efforts are fairly recognized and appreciated. By establishing clear criteria and processes for compensation decisions, organizations can uphold principles of fairness and equity, fostering trust and confidence among employees.

Moreover, compensation serves as a powerful motivator, driving individuals and teams to consistently strive for excellence. When employees feel that their efforts are valued and appreciated, they are more likely to remain engaged and motivated in their work. Recognition of dedication, innovation, and sustained effort not only boosts morale but also encourages continued commitment to organizational goals and objectives.

Promotions are a tangible form of recognition that signal career advancement and growth opportunities within an organization. By promoting employees based on merit and performance, organizations not only reward past contributions but also inspire future excellence. Promotions demonstrate a commitment to employee development and create a pathway for advancement, encouraging individuals to invest in their professional growth and skill development.

Bonuses are another effective means of recognizing exceptional performance and contributions. Whether tied to individual achievements or collective goals, bonuses provide tangible rewards that motivate employees to exceed expectations and deliver exceptional results. Additionally, bonuses can be customized to align with organizational objectives, incentivizing behaviors and outcomes that drive business success. Through strategic bonus programs, organizations can reinforce desired behaviors and outcomes, driving performance and fostering a culture of excellence.

Understanding Compensation

Compensation serves as a tangible expression of appreciation for the efforts and dedication demonstrated by individuals in the pursuit of organizational goals. Beyond monetary rewards, compensation encompasses various forms of recognition tailored to the diverse needs and preferences of employees. From public accolades and performance bonuses to professional development opportunities and flexible work arrangements, effective compensation strategies acknowledge the multidimensional nature of employee contributions and seek to align rewards with individual aspirations and organizational objectives.

The Role of Compensation in Achievement

At its core, compensation plays a crucial role in motivating individuals and teams to consistently strive for excellence in their endeavors. While financial incentives are important motivators, non-monetary rewards such as public recognition and career advancement opportunities are equally impactful in driving engagement and commitment. By offering a diverse range of incentives, organizations can create a dynamic compensation framework that resonates with their workforce and fosters a culture of high performance and achievement.

Moreover, the importance of fairness and equity in compensation cannot be understated. Employees expect to be compensated fairly and equitably for their efforts, regardless of their role or level within the organization. Fair compensation practices not only promote trust and transparency but also foster a sense of belonging and inclusivity among employees. By ensuring that compensation is commensurate with contributions, organizations can mitigate feelings of resentment or inequity and cultivate a supportive and harmonious work environment conducive to productivity and collaboration.

Practical Applications of Compensation

Effective compensation strategies extend beyond monetary rewards to encompass a holistic approach to recognition and acknowledgment. By incorporating non-financial incentives such as public praise, career development opportunities, and work-life balance initiatives, organizations can create a culture of appreciation that enhances employee morale and engagement. Additionally, transparent communication about compensation policies and practices fosters trust and confidence in organizational leadership, further reinforcing a positive work culture.

Case Studies: Real-World Examples of Effective Compensation:

To illustrate the transformative impact of compensation, let us examine a few real-world examples:

1. **Google:** Known for its innovative approach to compensation, Google offers a comprehensive package of benefits and perks to its employees, including competitive salaries, generous bonuses, and stock options. Additionally, Google has a peer recognition program where employees can nominate their colleagues for "spot awards" to recognize their outstanding contributions to the company.

2. **Southwest Airlines:** Southwest Airlines has a unique culture of appreciation known as "Living the Southwest Way." Employees are encouraged to recognize and celebrate each other's achievements through a variety of channels, including company-wide meetings,

social media shoutouts, and handwritten notes from leadership.

3. **Charity**: Water: Charity: Water, a nonprofit organization dedicated to providing clean and safe drinking water to people in developing countries, places a strong emphasis on donor appreciation. The organization regularly sends personalized thank-you notes and updates to its donors, recognizing their generosity and the impact of their contributions on the lives of others.

4. **Netflix:** Netflix is known for its unique compensation approach, which includes high salaries, generous stock options, and a culture of freedom and responsibility. The company offers competitive compensation packages to attract top talent and incentivizes performance through bonuses and stock grants tied to individual and company-wide achievements.

5. **Salesforce**: Salesforce has a strong commitment to employee success, offering a range of compensation incentives, including competitive salaries, performance-based bonuses, and stock options. The company also provides extensive benefits, such as healthcare coverage, wellness programs, and professional development opportunities, to support employee well-being and career growth.

6. **Microsoft:** Microsoft's compensation strategy focuses on rewarding employees for

their contributions to the company's success. In addition to competitive salaries and bonuses, Microsoft offers stock awards and performance-based incentives to motivate employees and align their interests with those of the organization.

7. **Procter & Gamble:** Procter & Gamble (P&G) values its employees' contributions and invests in their success through competitive compensation packages and performance-based incentives. P&G offers a range of benefits, including healthcare coverage, retirement plans, and tuition reimbursement, to support employee well-being and professional development.

8. **Apple:** Apple is known for its generous compensation packages, which include competitive salaries, bonuses, and stock options. The company also provides extensive benefits, such as health and wellness programs, employee discounts, and tuition assistance, to attract and retain top talent.

9. **Facebook:** Facebook offers competitive compensation packages, including high salaries, bonuses, and stock grants, to attract and retain top talent in the tech industry. The company also provides comprehensive benefits, such as healthcare coverage, retirement plans, and parental leave, to support employee well-being and work-life balance.

10. **Intel:** Intel rewards employees for their contributions to the company's success through competitive compensation packages, including salaries, bonuses, and stock options. The company also offers a range of benefits, such as healthcare coverage, retirement plans, and employee assistance programs, to support employee well-being and professional development.

11. **Cisco:** Cisco values its employees' contributions and invests in their success through competitive compensation packages and performance-based incentives. The company also provides extensive benefits, such as healthcare coverage, retirement plans, and professional development opportunities, to support employee well-being and career growth.

12. **Amazon:** Amazon offers competitive compensation packages, including high salaries, bonuses, and stock options, to attract and retain top talent. The company also provides comprehensive benefits, such as healthcare coverage, retirement plans, and employee discounts, to support employee well-being and work-life balance.

13. **LinkedIn:** LinkedIn rewards employees for their contributions to the company's success through competitive compensation packages, including salaries, bonuses, and stock grants. The company also offers a range of benefits, such as healthcare coverage, retirement

plans, and professional development opportunities, to support employee well-being and career growth.

14. **Adobe:** Adobe values its employees' contributions and invests in their success through competitive compensation packages and performance-based incentives. The company also provides extensive benefits, such as healthcare coverage, retirement plans, and employee wellness programs, to support employee well-being and professional development.

15. **Twitter:** Twitter offers competitive compensation packages, including salaries, bonuses, and stock options, to attract and retain top talent in the tech industry. The company also provides comprehensive benefits, such as healthcare coverage, retirement plans, and parental leave, to support employee well-being and work-life balance.

16. **Airbnb:** Airbnb values its employees' contributions and invests in their success through competitive compensation packages and performance-based incentives. The company also provides extensive benefits, such as healthcare coverage, retirement plans, and employee wellness programs, to support employee well-being and professional development.

17. **Uber:** Uber rewards employees for their contributions to the company's success

through competitive compensation packages, including salaries, bonuses, and stock grants. The company also offers a range of benefits, such as healthcare coverage, retirement plans, and employee discounts, to support employee well-being and work-life balance.

18. **IBM:** IBM values its employees' contributions and invests in their success through competitive compensation packages and performance-based incentives. The company also provides extensive benefits, such as healthcare coverage, retirement plans, and employee wellness programs, to support employee well-being and professional development.

19. **Tesla:** Tesla offers competitive compensation packages, including salaries, bonuses, and stock options, to attract and retain top talent in the automotive and technology industries. The company also provides comprehensive benefits, such as healthcare coverage, retirement plans, and employee discounts, to support employee well-being and work-life balance.

20. **PayPal**: PayPal rewards employees for their contributions to the company's success through competitive compensation packages, including salaries, bonuses, and stock grants. The company also offers a range of benefits, such as healthcare coverage, retirement plans, and employee wellness programs, to

support employee well-being and professional development.

Challenges and Opportunities in Cultivating Compensation:

Despite its many benefits, cultivating a culture of compensation can present challenges, particularly in large organizations or in environments where recognition is not prioritized. Additionally, ensuring that compensation is genuine and meaningful requires a nuanced understanding of individual preferences and motivations. Moreover, in diverse and multicultural settings, it is essential to recognize and respect cultural differences in expressions of compensation, ensuring that all individuals feel valued and respected.

Furthermore, the fast-paced nature of modern work environments can make it easy to overlook the importance of compensation in the pursuit of success. In a world where instant gratification and tangible outcomes are often prioritized, the intangible benefits of compensation may be undervalued or overlooked. However, by taking the time to recognize and reward contributions, organizations can cultivate a culture of compensation that fosters mutual respect, trust, and collaboration.

Compensation serves as a cornerstone of achievement, recognizing and rewarding contributions in the journey towards success. By acknowledging the intrinsic link between effort and reward, compensation reinforces a culture of appreciation that enhances motivation, engagement, and organizational performance. As the sixth pillar of success, compensation embodies the power of recognition and acknowledgment in creating a positive work environment where employees feel valued, appreciated, and empowered to contribute their best efforts towards achieving shared goals and aspirations.

CHAPTER SEVEN

Pillar 7: Celebration - Culminating in Joyous Acknowledgment

The final pillar, celebration, marks the culmination of the achievement journey. It involves the acknowledgment and enjoyment of successful outcomes or milestones achieved. Celebration is not just a momentary pause but a deliberate act of savoring the fruits of labor, fostering a sense of accomplishment, and instilling a positive and celebratory culture.

Celebration may take various forms, from formal ceremonies and events to simple expressions of gratitude. It serves as a powerful motivator, providing individuals and organizations with the opportunity to reflect on their journey, express appreciation for collective efforts, and recharge for future endeavors. The seventh pillar emphasizes the importance of joyous acknowledgment, ensuring that achievements are not only recognized but also enjoyed.

In the journey towards achievement, the seventh pillar, celebration, serves as a pivotal moment of reflection and recognition. It marks the culmination of efforts and milestones achieved, offering an opportunity to acknowledge success and foster a culture of joyous acknowledgment. This comprehensive exploration examine the critical nature of celebration, its transformative impact on morale and motivation, and its crucial role in instilling a positive and celebratory culture within individuals and organizations.

Celebration serves as a crucial component in reinforcing a positive organizational culture. By actively acknowledging and commemorating achievements, organizations can foster a sense of pride and camaraderie among employees. When individuals feel valued and appreciated for their contributions, they are more likely to remain engaged, motivated, and committed to organizational goals. Moreover, celebration provides an opportunity for leaders to publicly recognize and thank employees for their hard work, dedication, and accomplishments, which can boost morale and enhance employee satisfaction.

Furthermore, celebration acts as a form of social reinforcement, strengthening interpersonal relationships and promoting teamwork within organizations. When employees come together to celebrate shared successes, it creates a sense of unity and solidarity. Team celebrations provide an opportunity for individuals to bond, build trust, and collaborate more effectively in the future. By fostering a culture of celebration, organizations can cultivate a supportive and inclusive environment where teamwork is valued and encouraged.

In addition to its internal benefits, celebration also has external implications for organizations. Publicly acknowledging achievements can enhance an organization's reputation and brand image, making it more attractive to prospective employees, customers, and partners. When organizations celebrate their successes openly, it demonstrates confidence, competence, and a commitment to excellence, which can positively influence stakeholders' perceptions and decisions. Moreover, celebrating milestones and accomplishments can help organizations stand out in competitive markets, differentiate themselves from rivals, and position themselves as industry leaders.

Celebration also plays a vital role in promoting innovation and creativity within organizations. By recognizing and rewarding successful outcomes, organizations can inspire employees to take risks, experiment with new ideas, and push the boundaries of conventional thinking. When individuals feel supported and valued, they are more likely to engage in creative problem-solving and contribute innovative solutions to challenges. By celebrating innovation and creativity, organizations can foster a culture of continuous improvement and adaptability, driving long-term success and sustainability.

Ultimately, celebration serves as a reminder of the collective efforts and achievements that have led to success. It provides an opportunity for individuals and organizations to pause, reflect, and express gratitude for the journey traveled and the milestones achieved along the way. By embracing celebration as the final pillar of achievement, organizations can cultivate a culture of positivity, resilience, and appreciation, ensuring that successes are not only recognized but also cherished and celebrated.

Understanding Celebration

Celebration is more than just a momentary pause; it is a deliberate act of savoring the fruits of labor and acknowledging the journey towards success. This pillar emphasizes the importance of joyous acknowledgment, where achievements are celebrated and shared with enthusiasm and gratitude. Celebration serves as a powerful motivator, providing individuals and organizations with the opportunity to reflect on their accomplishments, express appreciation for collective efforts, and recharge for future endeavors.

The Role of Celebration in Achievement

At its core, celebration fosters a sense of accomplishment and pride among individuals and teams. By acknowledging success and milestones achieved, celebration reinforces the value of hard work, dedication, and perseverance. Moreover, celebration serves as a catalyst for continued growth and progress, as it provides an opportunity to reflect on lessons learned and set new goals for the future. In organizations, a culture of celebration contributes to employee engagement, satisfaction, and retention, ultimately driving greater productivity and performance.

Practical Applications of Celebration

Celebration can take various forms, ranging from formal ceremonies and events to simple expressions of gratitude and appreciation. Within organizations, leaders can cultivate a culture of celebration by recognizing achievements through employee awards, team outings, and appreciation events. Additionally, regular team meetings or huddles can serve as opportunities to celebrate successes, share accomplishments, and express gratitude for collective efforts.

Furthermore, celebration extends beyond the workplace to encompass personal achievements and milestones. Individuals can celebrate their accomplishments by setting aside time for self-reflection, expressing gratitude for support received, and indulging in activities that bring joy and fulfillment. Whether it's completing a project, reaching a personal goal, or overcoming a challenge, celebration provides an opportunity to acknowledge progress and celebrate success in all aspects of life.

Case Studies: Real-World Examples of Effective Celebration

To illustrate the transformative impact of celebration, let us examine a few real-world examples:

1. **Google:** Google is known for its vibrant and inclusive culture, which emphasizes the importance of celebrating success and milestones. The company regularly hosts themed parties, team outings, and recognition events to acknowledge achievements and foster a sense of camaraderie among employees.
2. **NASA:** NASA's mission control centers around the world celebrate major milestones in space exploration, such as successful launches, landings, and scientific discoveries. These celebrations not only recognize the achievements of the entire team but also inspire future generations to pursue careers in space exploration.
3. **Nonprofit Organizations:** Nonprofit organizations often rely on celebration as a means of recognizing the contributions of volunteers, donors, and supporters. Events such as donor appreciation dinners, volunteer recognition ceremonies, and fundraising galas provide opportunities to celebrate

achievements and express gratitude for the collective effort.

4. **Salesforce:** Salesforce, a leading cloud-based software company, is renowned for its vibrant culture of celebration. The company organizes annual events like "Dreamforce," a massive conference that brings together customers, partners, and employees to celebrate achievements, share insights, and foster collaboration. Additionally, Salesforce hosts regular team-building activities, themed parties, and recognition ceremonies to acknowledge individual and team accomplishments.

5. **Nike:** Nike, a global sportswear giant, prioritizes celebration as a means of fostering camaraderie and motivation among employees. The company hosts "Nike Days," where employees are encouraged to participate in sports activities and team-building exercises. Moreover, Nike celebrates product launches, milestones, and achievements through company-wide events, award ceremonies, and social media campaigns, creating a culture of pride and accomplishment.

6. **Zappos:** Zappos, an online retailer known for its exceptional customer service, places a strong emphasis on celebrating achievements and milestones. The company hosts monthly "All-Hands" meetings where employees are recognized for their contributions, and

success stories are shared with the entire organization. Additionally, Zappos encourages employees to celebrate personal milestones, such as birthdays and work anniversaries, fostering a sense of community and appreciation.

7. **Pixar:** Pixar Animation Studios, renowned for its groundbreaking films, celebrates the completion of each project with a tradition called "The Wrap Party." These parties are elaborate events where employees come together to celebrate the successful completion of a film, share stories, and reflect on the journey. Pixar's commitment to celebrating success creates a supportive and collaborative work environment that inspires creativity and innovation.

8. **Starbucks:** Starbucks, the global coffee chain, celebrates its employees' achievements through various recognition programs and events. The company hosts "Partner Appreciation Days," where employees are treated to special perks, discounts, and recognition ceremonies. Moreover, Starbucks encourages customers to participate in celebrations through initiatives like "National Coffee Day," where free coffee is offered to customers as a token of appreciation.

9. **Netflix:** Netflix, the streaming entertainment powerhouse, celebrates the success of its original content through events

like "Premiere Parties" and award ceremonies. These events bring together cast, crew, and executives to celebrate the launch of new shows and movies. Additionally, Netflix recognizes employees' contributions through internal programs like "Employee of the Month" and "Spotlight Awards," fostering a culture of appreciation and recognition.

10. **The Coca-Cola Company:** The Coca-Cola Company, a global beverage giant, celebrates its achievements through initiatives like "Founders Day," which commemorates the company's founding anniversary. Employees participate in events like community service projects, team-building activities, and celebratory gatherings to honor the company's heritage and successes. Coca-Cola also recognizes employees' contributions through awards, incentives, and recognition programs.

11. **Amazon:** Amazon, the e-commerce behemoth, celebrates its achievements through annual events like "Prime Day" and "Amazon Day," where customers are treated to exclusive deals and promotions. Internally, Amazon acknowledges employees' contributions through programs like "Pioneer Awards" and "Career Choice," which provide recognition and support for career development. Additionally, Amazon hosts

team-building events, parties, and outings to celebrate milestones and successes.

12. **Walt Disney Company:** The Walt Disney Company, known for its theme parks, films, and entertainment franchises, celebrates its achievements through events like "Disneyland Anniversary" and "D23 Expo," where fans and employees come together to celebrate Disney's legacy and future projects. Additionally, Disney recognizes employees' contributions through programs like "Partners in Excellence" and "Disney Legends," which honor exemplary service and dedication.

13. **Microsoft:** Microsoft, a leading technology company, celebrates its achievements through events like "Microsoft Ignite" and "Build Conference," where developers, partners, and customers gather to celebrate innovation and technology advancements. Internally, Microsoft acknowledges employees' contributions through programs like "Impact Awards" and "Hackathons," which recognize excellence and creativity. Additionally, Microsoft hosts team-building events, hackathons, and social gatherings to celebrate successes and foster collaboration.

14. **Hershey's:** Hershey's, the iconic chocolate manufacturer, celebrates its achievements through events like "National Chocolate Day" and "Hershey's Anniversary," where customers are treated to special promotions

and events. Internally, Hershey's recognizes employees' contributions through programs like "Employee of the Month" and "Recognition Awards," which honor outstanding performance and dedication. Additionally, Hershey's hosts team-building events, employee appreciation days, and family picnics to celebrate successes and foster a sense of community.

15. **Harley-Davidson:** Harley-Davidson, the legendary motorcycle manufacturer, celebrates its achievements through events like "Harley-Davidson Anniversary" and "Bike Week," where enthusiasts come together to celebrate the brand's heritage and lifestyle. Internally, Harley-Davidson acknowledges employees' contributions through programs like "Employee Recognition Awards" and "President's Club," which recognize excellence and dedication. Additionally, Harley-Davidson hosts employee appreciation events, team-building activities, and motorcycle rallies to celebrate successes and strengthen camaraderie.

16. **Red Bull:** Red Bull, the energy drink company, celebrates its achievements through events like "Red Bull Flugtag" and "Red Bull Rampage," where athletes and adrenaline junkies showcase their skills and creativity. Internally, Red Bull acknowledges employees' contributions through programs like "Wings for Excellence" and "Red Bull

Hero Awards," which recognize outstanding performance and dedication. Additionally, Red Bull hosts team-building events, employee appreciation parties, and extreme sports competitions to celebrate successes and inspire greatness.

17. **Patagonia:** Patagonia, the outdoor apparel brand, celebrates its achievements through events like "Patagonia Earth Day" and "Worn Wear Tour," where customers and employees come together to celebrate sustainability and outdoor adventure. Internally, Patagonia acknowledges employees' contributions through programs like "Employee Environmental Awards" and "Outstanding Service Awards," which recognize excellence and dedication. Additionally, Patagonia hosts employee appreciation events, volunteer outings, and environmental clean-up initiatives to celebrate successes and promote environmental stewardship.

18. **Tesla:** Tesla, the electric vehicle manufacturer, celebrates its achievements through events like "Tesla Delivery Day" and "Tesla Autonomy Day," where customers and enthusiasts come together to celebrate innovation and technology. Internally, Tesla acknowledges employees' contributions through programs like "Drive to Excellence" and "Tesla Top Performers," which recognize outstanding performance and dedication. Additionally, Tesla hosts team-building

events, employee appreciation dinners, and product launch parties to celebrate successes and foster collaboration.

19. **Lululemon:** Lululemon, the athletic apparel retailer, celebrates its achievements through events like "Lululemon Yoga Fest" and "Lululemon Run Club," where customers and employees come together to celebrate health and wellness. Internally, Lululemon acknowledges employees' contributions through programs like "Lululemon Ambassador Awards" and "Sweat Collective Recognition," which recognize excellence and dedication. Additionally, Lululemon hosts employee appreciation events, fitness challenges, and wellness retreats to celebrate successes and promote a healthy lifestyle.

20. **REI:** REI, the outdoor recreation retailer, celebrates its achievements through events like "REI Anniversary Sale" and "REI Outdoor School," where customers and employees come together to celebrate outdoor adventure and conservation. Internally, REI acknowledges employees' contributions through programs like "REI Co-op Awards" **and** "Employee of the Year," which recognize excellence and dedication. Additionally, REI hosts employee appreciation events, outdoor excursions, and environmental stewardship projects to celebrate successes and promote outdoor recreation.

Challenges and Opportunities in Cultivating Celebration

Despite its many benefits, cultivating a culture of celebration can present challenges, particularly in fast-paced and high-pressure environments. Organizations may struggle to find time and resources to dedicate to celebration, especially during busy periods or when faced with budget constraints. Additionally, ensuring that celebration is inclusive and accessible to all members of the organization requires careful planning and consideration of diverse preferences and needs.

Moreover, the virtual nature of work in today's digital age presents new opportunities and challenges for celebrating success. With remote and distributed teams becoming increasingly common, organizations must find innovative ways to foster a sense of connection and camaraderie among employees. Virtual celebrations, such as online recognition ceremonies, digital awards, and virtual team-building activities, offer opportunities to celebrate success and build community across geographical boundaries.

Celebration serves as a cornerstone of achievement, marking the culmination of efforts and milestones achieved on the journey towards success. By cultivating a culture of joyous acknowledgment, individuals and organizations can foster a sense of pride, appreciation, and belonging. Celebration provides an opportunity to reflect on accomplishments, express gratitude for collective efforts, and recharge for future endeavors. As the seventh pillar of achievement, celebration embodies the power of recognition and appreciation in creating a positive and celebratory culture that inspires greatness and drives sustained success.

"The Seven Pillars of Achievement" presents a holistic framework that guides individuals and organizations through a deliberate and intentional journey towards success. Each pillar represents a crucial phase in the process, from the identification of challenges or opportunities to the joyous celebration of achievements. This comprehensive approach ensures that achievement is not a happenstance but a result of conscious efforts, informed decisions, and a commitment to continuous growth. Through the seamless integration of these pillars, this blueprint for success provides a roadmap for navigating the complexities of the achievement journey and unlocking the full potential of individuals and organizations alike.

CHAPTER EIGHT

Chronicles of Visionaries: Exploring the Impact of the Seven Pillars of Achievement on Great Innovators, Transformers, Disruptors, and Influencers.

Throughout history, humanity has been witnessed to the remarkable achievements of individuals who have left an indelible mark on the world. From groundbreaking innovations to profound social change, these visionaries have reshaped our understanding of what is possible and inspired generations to reach for greatness. At the core of their success lies a set of guiding principles, which we can distill into the seven pillars of achievement: Identification, Action, Education, Application, Appreciation, Compensation, and Celebration.

Identification

The journey of achievement begins with identification – the ability to recognize opportunities or challenges that demand attention. Across diverse fields and disciplines, great men and women have demonstrated a keen sense of observation and foresight in identifying areas ripe for exploration and growth. Whether it was John D. Rockefeller identifying the potential of the oil industry in the late

19th century or Margaret Thatcher recognizing the need for economic reform in 1980s Britain, these individuals possessed an innate ability to discern the contours of change and act upon them.

Action

Identifying opportunities is only the first step; true progress is made through action. Visionaries like Bill Gates and Elon Musk have exemplified this pillar by translating their ideas into tangible outcomes through strategic planning and decisive execution. By taking bold action, they have transformed industries and redefined the boundaries of what is possible, inspiring others to follow in their footsteps.

Education

Education serves as the cornerstone of achievement, providing individuals with the knowledge and skills needed to navigate the complexities of their chosen field. From the academic rigor of Barack Obama to the entrepreneurial spirit of Jeff Bezos, great achievers have recognized the importance of continuous learning and self-improvement. By investing in their education, they have equipped themselves with the tools necessary to overcome obstacles and seize opportunities.

Application

Knowledge alone is not enough; it must be applied effectively to bring about meaningful change. Visionaries like Michael Jordan and Pele have demonstrated the power of application by honing their craft through relentless practice and dedication. By applying their skills in real-world contexts, they have achieved unparalleled success and inspired millions around the world to pursue their passions with unwavering determination.

Appreciation

Achievement is not a solitary endeavor; it is the result of collective effort and collaboration. Great men and women understand the importance of appreciation – recognizing and valuing the contributions of others along the way. Whether it is through acknowledging the support of friends and family or expressing gratitude to colleagues and mentors, appreciation fosters a culture of mutual respect and camaraderie that is essential for long-term success.

Compensation

Fair compensation is essential for sustaining motivation and incentivizing continued effort. Leaders like Martin Luther King Jr. and Colin Powell have fought tirelessly for justice and equality, recognizing the importance of just compensation for all individuals. By advocating for fair treatment and equitable opportunities, they have paved the way for a more inclusive and prosperous society.

Celebration

Finally, achievement is not just about reaching the destination; it is about savoring the journey and celebrating the milestones along the way. From the jubilant performances of The Beatles to the uplifting message of Bob Marley, great men and women have understood the importance of celebration in fostering a sense of joy and fulfillment. By taking the time to acknowledge and celebrate their achievements, they have inspired others to do the same and create a legacy that endures for generations to come.

The stories of these great men and women serve as a testament to the transformative power of the seven pillars of achievement. By embodying these principles in their lives and work, they have not only achieved greatness but also inspired others to reach for their own dreams and aspirations. As we embark on our own journey of achievement, may we draw inspiration from their example and strive to make our mark on the world in our own unique way.

Bill Gates: A Journey of Achievement and Philanthropy

Bill Gates, co-founder of Microsoft Corporation and one of the world's most influential philanthropists, is a testament to the power of vision, perseverance, and commitment to making a difference. His life and journey exemplify the seven pillars of achievement, as he navigated challenges, seized opportunities, and ultimately transformed the world of technology while dedicating himself to philanthropic endeavors that aim to solve some of the world's most pressing issues.

Pillar 1: Identification - Unveiling the Essence

Bill Gates's journey began with a keen sense of identification. Born on October 28, 1955, in Seattle, Washington, Gates displayed an early aptitude for mathematics and programming. Identifying his passion for technology and computer programming, Gates immersed himself in the world of computers at a young age. He recognized the potential of personal computing to revolutionize the way people work and communicate, laying the groundwork for his future endeavors in the field.

Pillar 2: Action - Bridging Vision and Reality

Driven by his vision of a future where computers would be accessible to everyone, Gates took decisive action. In 1975, while still a student at Harvard University, he co-founded Microsoft with his childhood friend Paul Allen. Despite facing numerous challenges and setbacks, including fierce competition and legal battles, Gates remained undeterred in his pursuit of success. His strategic approach to business, combined with his unwavering determination, allowed Microsoft to emerge as a dominant force in the technology industry.

Pillar 3: Education - Empowering Through Knowledge

Throughout his career, Gates recognized the importance of continuous learning and knowledge acquisition. Despite dropping out of Harvard to focus on Microsoft full-time, Gates remained committed to expanding his knowledge and understanding of technology and business. He immersed himself in the intricacies of software development, constantly seeking to innovate and improve Microsoft's products. Additionally, Gates recognized the value of education in empowering individuals and communities, leading him to establish the Bill & Melinda Gates Foundation, which is dedicated to improving global health and education.

Pillar 4: Application - Transforming Knowledge into Action

Armed with his knowledge and expertise, Gates applied his insights to drive innovation and create real-world impact. Under his leadership, Microsoft developed groundbreaking software products such as MS-DOS and Windows, which revolutionized personal computing and propelled the company to unprecedented success. Gates's ability to translate theoretical knowledge into practical solutions cemented Microsoft's position as a technology powerhouse and solidified his reputation as a visionary leader.

Pillar 5: Appreciation - Cultivating Recognition and Acknowledgment

Gates understood the importance of appreciation in fostering a positive and supportive environment. Throughout his tenure at Microsoft, he recognized the contributions of his employees and valued their efforts in driving the company's success. Gates's leadership style emphasized collaboration, teamwork, and mutual respect, creating a culture where employees felt valued and motivated to excel. Additionally, through the Bill & Melinda Gates Foundation, Gates expressed appreciation for the efforts of individuals and organizations working to address global challenges, recognizing their contributions to positive change.

Pillar 6: Compensation - Recognizing and Rewarding Contributions

As a proponent of fair compensation and recognition, Gates ensured that employees at Microsoft were appropriately rewarded for their contributions. He implemented incentive programs, performance bonuses, and stock options to incentivize excellence and foster a sense of ownership among employees. Gates recognized the intrinsic link between effort and reward, acknowledging the importance of recognizing and celebrating achievements in driving motivation and engagement.

Pillar 7: Celebration - Culminating in Joyous Acknowledgment

Gates's journey culminates in celebration, as he reflects on his achievements and the impact he has made on the world. Through Microsoft, Gates revolutionized the technology industry, democratizing access to computing and transforming the way people work, communicate, and connect. Furthermore, through the Bill & Melinda Gates Foundation, Gates has dedicated himself to philanthropy, tackling some of the world's most pressing issues, including global health, education, and poverty alleviation. As he celebrates his successes, Gates remains committed to his mission of making the world a better place for future generations.

Bill Gates's life and journey exemplify the seven pillars of achievement, from his early identification of a passion for technology to his relentless pursuit of success and his dedication to making a difference through philanthropy. His story serves as an inspiration to aspiring entrepreneurs, innovators, and philanthropists around the world, demonstrating the transformative power of vision, action, and commitment to positive change. As Gates continues to shape the future through his endeavors, his legacy will endure as a testament to the enduring impact of achievement and the importance of giving back to society.

John D. Rockefeller: The Journey of a Titan

John D. Rockefeller, the American industrialist and philanthropist, was one of the most influential figures of the late 19th and early 20th centuries. Born on July 8, 1839, in Richford, New York, Rockefeller rose from modest beginnings to become the founder of Standard Oil Company and one of the wealthiest individuals in history. His journey of achievement is a testament to the power of vision, determination, and strategic thinking. Through the lens of the seven pillars of achievement, we explore Rockefeller's life and legacy, examining the key moments and guiding principles that shaped his extraordinary success.

Pillar 1: Identification - Unveiling the Essence

John D. Rockefeller's journey of achievement began with a keen sense of identification. From a young age, he demonstrated a knack for business and a keen understanding of the oil industry. Recognizing the potential for growth and consolidation in the oil refining business, Rockefeller set out to build an empire that would revolutionize the industry. He identified inefficiencies in the existing market structure and saw an opportunity to streamline operations and maximize profits through vertical integration.

Pillar 2: Action - Bridging Vision and Reality

Armed with his vision of creating a vertically integrated oil company, John D. Rockefeller took decisive action to turn his dreams into reality. In 1870, he founded Standard Oil Company, which would eventually become one of the largest and most powerful corporations in the world. Through a series of strategic acquisitions and aggressive expansion efforts, Rockefeller consolidated control over nearly all aspects of the oil industry, from drilling and refining to transportation and marketing. His relentless pursuit of efficiency and economies of scale transformed the oil business and solidified his reputation as a titan of industry.

Pillar 3: Education - Empowering Through Knowledge

Education played a crucial role in John D. Rockefeller's journey of achievement. Despite lacking a formal education, Rockefeller possessed a voracious appetite for learning and a keen intellect. He immersed himself in the study of business and finance, constantly seeking out new information and insights to inform his decision-making. Rockefeller was a firm believer in the power of knowledge to drive success, and he surrounded himself with a team of experts and advisors who helped him navigate the complexities of the business world.

Pillar 4: Application - Transforming Knowledge into Action

John D. Rockefeller's ability to translate knowledge into action was a hallmark of his success. He was a master strategist who understood the importance of careful planning and execution. Rockefeller applied his insights and expertise to every aspect of his business, from negotiating deals and managing operations to developing innovative marketing strategies. His disciplined approach to business allowed him to stay ahead of his competitors and achieve unprecedented levels of success in the oil industry.

Pillar 5: Appreciation - Cultivating Recognition and Acknowledgment

Throughout his career, John D. Rockefeller remained grounded in humility and gratitude. He understood the importance of building strong relationships and treating others with respect and appreciation. Rockefeller valued the contributions of his employees and business partners, recognizing that their hard work and dedication were essential to the success of Standard Oil. He was known for his fair and equitable treatment of workers and his commitment to giving back to the communities where his company operated.

Pillar 6: Compensation - Recognizing and Rewarding Contributions

While financial compensation played a role in John D. Rockefeller's journey, his greatest rewards came from the satisfaction of achieving his goals and making a positive impact on the world. Rockefeller was famously frugal and lived modestly despite his immense wealth. He believed in the importance of using his resources to improve the lives of others, and he dedicated much of his fortune to philanthropic endeavors, including education, healthcare, and scientific research. Rockefeller's philanthropy left a lasting legacy that continues to benefit society to this day.

Pillar 7: Celebration - Culminating in Joyous Acknowledgment

John D. Rockefeller's journey of achievement was marked by countless moments of celebration and acknowledgment. From the early successes of Standard Oil to his later philanthropic efforts, Rockefeller took pride in his accomplishments and reveled in the joy of making a difference in the world. He celebrated the achievements of his employees and business partners and took pleasure in seeing his vision come to fruition. Rockefeller's life and legacy serve as a reminder of the power of perseverance, determination, and a relentless pursuit of excellence.

John D. Rockefeller's journey of achievement is a testament to the transformative power of vision, determination, and strategic thinking. Through the seven pillars of achievement, Rockefeller built an empire that revolutionized the oil industry and left an indelible mark on the world. His legacy continues to inspire generations of entrepreneurs and business leaders to dream big, take decisive action, and make a positive impact on the world. As we reflect on Rockefeller's remarkable journey, let us celebrate his achievements and draw inspiration from his enduring legacy of innovation, integrity, and philanthropy.

Jeff Bezos: A Journey of Innovation and Leadership

Jeff Bezos, the founder of Amazon.com and one of the most prominent entrepreneurs of the 21st century, embodies the seven pillars of achievement in his remarkable life journey. From humble beginnings to becoming the world's richest person, Bezos's story is a testament to vision, perseverance, and innovation. This narrative explores Bezos's life and achievements through the lens of the seven pillars, highlighting the pivotal moments and guiding principles that shaped his journey to success.

Pillar 1: Identification - Unveiling the Essence

Jeff Bezos was born on January 12, 1964, in Albuquerque, New Mexico. From an early age, Bezos displayed a keen interest in science and technology. After graduating from Princeton University with degrees in computer science and electrical engineering, Bezos embarked on a career in finance, working for firms such as Fitel, Bankers Trust, and D. E. Shaw & Co. It was during his time at D. E. Shaw & Co. that Bezos identified a burgeoning opportunity in the burgeoning e-commerce industry. Recognizing the potential of the internet to revolutionize retail, Bezos decided to pursue his entrepreneurial ambitions and founded Amazon.com in 1994.

Pillar 2: Action - Bridging Vision and Reality

Driven by his vision of creating the world's largest online marketplace, Bezos took decisive action to bring his idea to fruition. He left his lucrative job at D. E. Shaw & Co. and moved to Seattle to launch Amazon.com from his garage. Despite facing skepticism and challenges from traditional retailers, Bezos remained steadfast in his belief in the transformative power of e-commerce. He focused on building a customer-centric business model, offering a wide selection of products, competitive prices, and unparalleled convenience. Bezos's boldness and determination paid off, as Amazon.com quickly gained traction and became a dominant force in the retail industry.

Pillar 3: Education - Empowering Through Knowledge

Throughout his entrepreneurial journey, Bezos recognized the importance of continuous learning and knowledge acquisition. He immersed himself in the intricacies of technology, business strategy, and customer behavior, constantly seeking to innovate and improve Amazon's offerings. Bezos also valued intellectual curiosity and encouraged a culture of experimentation and risk-taking within the company. Under his leadership, Amazon expanded beyond e-commerce into new areas such as cloud computing, artificial intelligence, and digital streaming, cementing its position as a technology powerhouse.

Pillar 4: Application - Transforming Knowledge into Action

Armed with his knowledge and insights, Bezos applied innovative thinking and strategic execution to drive Amazon's growth and success. He spearheaded initiatives such as Amazon Prime, which revolutionized online shopping by offering fast and free shipping to members. Bezos also led the development of Amazon Web Services (AWS), a cloud computing platform that has become a major revenue driver for the company. Through bold investments and acquisitions, Bezos transformed Amazon from an online bookstore into a diversified conglomerate with a global footprint.

Pillar 5: Appreciation - Cultivating Recognition and Acknowledgment

As a leader, Bezos understood the importance of appreciation in fostering a positive and motivated workforce. He valued the contributions of Amazon's employees and prioritized creating a supportive and inclusive work environment. Bezos also recognized the importance of customer satisfaction and was known for his relentless focus on delivering value and delighting customers. Through initiatives such as the Customer Obsession program, Bezos instilled a culture of customer-centricity within Amazon, driving loyalty and repeat business.

Pillar 6: Compensation - Recognizing and Rewarding Contributions

Bezos believed in recognizing and rewarding the contributions of Amazon's employees. He implemented innovative compensation and incentive programs to incentivize excellence and foster a culture of ownership and accountability. Bezos also valued long-term thinking and encouraged employees to think big and take risks. Through stock options and performance-based bonuses, Bezos ensured that employees were aligned with Amazon's long-term goals and motivated to deliver results.

Pillar 7: Celebration - Culminating in Joyous Acknowledgment

As Amazon grew and achieved milestones, Bezos celebrated the company's successes and milestones. He recognized the importance of acknowledging achievements and milestones along the way, whether it be the launch of a new product or the expansion into a new market. Bezos also celebrated the contributions of Amazon's customers and partners, recognizing their role in the company's success. Through annual events such as Prime Day and AWS re:Invent, Bezos brought together employees, customers, and stakeholders to celebrate Amazon's achievements and envision the future.

Jeff Bezos's life and journey exemplify the seven pillars of achievement, from his early identification of opportunities to his relentless pursuit of innovation and success. Through vision, perseverance, and leadership, Bezos transformed Amazon into one of the world's most valuable and influential companies, revolutionizing the retail industry and reshaping the way people shop, work, and live. As Bezos transitions to new endeavors, his legacy will endure as a testament to the enduring power of achievement and the transformative impact of visionary leadership.

Margaret Thatcher: A Journey of Leadership and Legacy

Margaret Thatcher, the Iron Lady of British politics, left an indelible mark on the world stage through her leadership, determination, and unwavering commitment to her principles. As the first female Prime Minister of the United Kingdom, Thatcher's life journey exemplifies the seven pillars of achievement. From her humble beginnings to her transformative tenure as Prime Minister, Thatcher's story serves as a beacon of inspiration for leaders and aspiring achievers worldwide. This narrative explores Thatcher's life and achievements through the lens of the seven pillars, shedding light on the guiding principles that shaped her journey to success.

Pillar 1: Identification - Unveiling the Essence

Margaret Thatcher was born on October 13, 1925, in Grantham, Lincolnshire, England. Raised in a modest household, Thatcher developed a strong work ethic and a deep sense of self-reliance from an early age. She excelled academically and won a scholarship to study chemistry at Oxford University, where she developed a keen interest in politics. After graduating, Thatcher pursued a career in law and later entered politics, serving as a Member of Parliament for Finchley for over two decades. Throughout her political career, Thatcher identified the essence of her vision: to restore Britain's economic strength, promote free-market principles, and confront the challenges facing the nation head-on.

Pillar 2: Action - Bridging Vision and Reality

Thatcher's ascent to the highest office in the land was marked by decisive action and unwavering determination. In 1979, she became the leader of the Conservative Party and was elected Prime Minister, making history as Britain's first female head of government. Thatcher wasted no time in implementing her bold vision for economic reform, famously declaring, "The lady's not for turning." She pursued an agenda of deregulation, privatization, and fiscal discipline, earning the nickname "The Iron Lady" for her uncompromising leadership style. Thatcher's actions transformed the British economy, revitalizing industries, curbing inflation, and restoring Britain's reputation as a global economic powerhouse.

Pillar 3: Education - Empowering Through Knowledge

Throughout her tenure as Prime Minister, Thatcher demonstrated a commitment to continuous learning and intellectual curiosity. She surrounded herself with a team of top advisors and economists, including Sir Geoffrey Howe and Sir Keith Joseph, who helped shape her policy agenda. Thatcher also valued the importance of education in empowering individuals and driving economic prosperity. She championed educational reforms, emphasizing choice, competition, and standards in schools. Thatcher's belief in the transformative power of education paved the way for initiatives such as the City Technology Colleges and the expansion of higher education opportunities for all.

Pillar 4: Application - Transforming Knowledge into Action

Armed with her knowledge and insights, Thatcher applied her principles with conviction and resolve. She confronted powerful vested interests, including trade unions and entrenched bureaucracy, to implement her agenda of reform. Thatcher's government privatized state-owned industries, deregulated financial markets, and curbed the power of labor unions, unleashing a wave of entrepreneurial energy and innovation. Her bold policies sparked a revival of the British economy, laying the groundwork for decades of sustained growth and prosperity.

Pillar 5: Appreciation - Cultivating Recognition and Acknowledgment

As a leader, Thatcher understood the importance of recognition and acknowledgment in motivating individuals and fostering a sense of purpose and commitment. She valued the contributions of her cabinet colleagues and the British people, recognizing their resilience and determination in the face of adversity. Thatcher also appreciated the sacrifices made by British servicemen and women, particularly during the Falklands War, where her decisive leadership restored Britain's sovereignty over the Falkland Islands. Through her speeches and actions, Thatcher instilled a sense of pride and patriotism in the British people, celebrating their achievements and resilience in times of triumph and adversity alike.

Pillar 6: Compensation - Recognizing and Rewarding Contributions

Thatcher believed in recognizing and rewarding the contributions of individuals who demonstrated excellence and dedication. She implemented policies to incentivize entrepreneurship and innovation, including tax cuts, enterprise zones, and incentives for small businesses. Thatcher also valued the importance of meritocracy and promoted individuals based on their abilities and achievements rather than their social background or connections. Her government's policies created opportunities for upward mobility and economic prosperity, rewarding hard work and ingenuity and fostering a culture of achievement and aspiration.

Pillar 7: Celebration - Culminating in Joyous Acknowledgment

Throughout her tenure as Prime Minister, Thatcher celebrated Britain's achievements and successes, from economic revitalization to victory in the Falklands War. She recognized the resilience and determination of the British people in overcoming adversity and achieving greatness. Thatcher's leadership inspired a sense of national pride and unity, fostering a culture of celebration and appreciation for Britain's accomplishments on the world stage.

Margaret Thatcher's life journey exemplifies the seven pillars of achievement, from her early identification of opportunities to her unwavering commitment to her principles and her transformative leadership as Prime Minister. Through vision, action, and determination, Thatcher revitalized the British economy, restored Britain's standing on the world stage, and inspired a generation of leaders. Her legacy endures as a testament to the enduring power of achievement and the transformative impact of principled leadership in shaping the course of history.

Barack Obama: A Journey of Leadership and Legacy

Barack Obama, the 44th President of the United States, is a towering figure in contemporary politics whose life journey exemplifies the seven pillars of achievement. From his early years to his historic presidency, Obama's story is one of resilience, leadership, and dedication to public service. This narrative explores Obama's life and achievements through the lens of the seven pillars, highlighting the pivotal moments and guiding principles that shaped his journey to the White House and beyond.

Pillar 1: Identification - Unveiling the Essence

Barack Hussein Obama II was born on August 4, 1961, in Honolulu, Hawaii. Raised by his mother and grandparents, Obama's multicultural upbringing instilled in him a deep sense of empathy and understanding of diverse perspectives. From a young age, Obama showed a keen interest in social justice and community activism, traits that would shape his future endeavors. After graduating from Columbia University and Harvard Law School, Obama embarked on a career in public service, working as a community organizer, civil rights attorney, and lecturer on constitutional law.

Pillar 2: Action - Bridging Vision and Reality

Driven by his vision of a more inclusive and equitable society, Obama took decisive action to bring about change. In 2004, he burst onto the national stage with a stirring keynote address at the Democratic National Convention, where he famously proclaimed, "There is not a liberal America and a conservative America—there is the United States of America." Inspired by his message of hope and unity, Obama launched his historic presidential campaign in 2007, vowing to build a grassroots movement to transform American politics. Despite facing skepticism and formidable opponents,

Obama's message resonated with millions of Americans, propelling him to victory in the 2008 presidential election.

Pillar 3: Education - Empowering Through Knowledge

Throughout his political career, Obama recognized the power of education as a catalyst for change and empowerment. As president, he prioritized initiatives to expand access to quality education, including the Affordable Care Act, which provided millions of Americans with affordable healthcare coverage. Obama also championed education reform efforts such as Race to the Top, which incentivized states to adopt rigorous standards and improve student outcomes. Additionally, Obama's administration invested in STEM education and vocational training programs to equip Americans with the skills needed to succeed in the 21st-century economy.

Pillar 4: Application - Transforming Knowledge into Action

Armed with his knowledge and insights, Obama applied innovative thinking and strategic execution to address pressing challenges facing the nation. In response to the global financial crisis of 2008, Obama enacted the American Recovery and Reinvestment Act, a stimulus package aimed at reviving the economy and creating jobs. He also prioritized environmental conservation and renewable energy, implementing regulations to combat climate change and promote clean energy innovation. Additionally, Obama pursued landmark healthcare reform with the passage of the Affordable Care Act, expanding access to healthcare coverage and protecting millions of Americans from discrimination based on pre-existing conditions.

Pillar 5: Appreciation - Cultivating Recognition and Acknowledgment

As a leader, Obama understood the importance of appreciation in fostering collaboration and unity. He valued the contributions of his fellow Americans and sought to recognize their efforts in advancing the common good. Throughout his presidency, Obama regularly expressed gratitude to the men and women serving in the armed forces, honoring their sacrifice and dedication to protecting the nation. He also celebrated the achievements of everyday Americans, from entrepreneurs and innovators to artists and activists, highlighting their stories as examples of the nation's resilience and diversity.

Pillar 6: Compensation - Recognizing and Rewarding Contributions

Obama believed in recognizing and rewarding the contributions of individuals and communities to the betterment of society. He implemented policies to support working families, including the expansion of tax credits for low-income households and increases in the minimum wage. Obama also advocated for equal pay for women and supported initiatives to close the gender pay gap. Additionally, he championed criminal justice reform efforts to address systemic inequalities in the legal system and promote fairness and equality under the law.

Pillar 7: Celebration - Culminating in Joyous Acknowledgment

Throughout his presidency, Obama celebrated the achievements and milestones of the American people, from the passage of landmark legislation to the commemoration of historic events. He marked significant occasions with speeches and ceremonies, honoring the contributions of individuals and communities to the nation's progress. Obama also celebrated cultural milestones, such as Black History Month and LGBTQ Pride Month, recognizing the rich tapestry of diversity that defines the American experience. As he concluded his presidency, Obama reflected on the nation's progress and expressed optimism for the future, emphasizing the importance of unity and collective action in addressing the challenges ahead.

Barack Obama's life and journey exemplify the seven pillars of achievement, from his early identification of opportunities to his transformative leadership as president. Through vision, perseverance, and a commitment to public service, Obama inspired millions of Americans to believe in the promise of a more perfect union. As he continues his work as a statesman, author, and advocate, Obama's legacy will endure as a testament to the enduring power of achievement and the transformative impact of visionary leadership.

Elon Musk: A Visionary's Journey of Innovation and Achievement

Elon Musk, the enigmatic entrepreneur and innovator, is a modern-day visionary whose life journey epitomizes the seven pillars of achievement. From his early ventures to his groundbreaking work in technology and space exploration, Musk's story is a testament to the power of determination, innovation, and relentless pursuit of ambitious goals. This narrative explores Musk's remarkable life and achievements through the lens of the seven pillars, highlighting the transformative impact of his visionary leadership on industries ranging from electric vehicles to space travel.

Pillar 1: Identification - Unveiling the Essence

Elon Reeve Musk was born on June 28, 1971, in Pretoria, South Africa. From an early age, Musk demonstrated a voracious appetite for knowledge and a keen interest in technology. As a child, he taught himself computer programming and developed a passion for science fiction and space exploration. Musk's insatiable curiosity and entrepreneurial spirit led him to identify opportunities for innovation and disruption in various industries, laying the groundwork for his future endeavors.

Pillar 2: Action - Bridging Vision and Reality

Driven by his vision of a sustainable future and humanity's expansion beyond Earth, Musk took bold action to bring his ideas to life. In 1995, he co-founded Zip2, a software company that provided online business directories and maps. Following the sale of Zip2, Musk co-founded X.com, an online payment company that later became PayPal, revolutionizing the way people conduct financial transactions. With the proceeds from PayPal, Musk went on to found SpaceX, Tesla, and SolarCity, each aimed at addressing critical challenges facing humanity, from climate change to space exploration.

Pillar 3: Education - Empowering Through Knowledge

Throughout his career, Musk has recognized the importance of continuous learning and knowledge acquisition in driving innovation and success.

Despite lacking formal education in aerospace engineering, Musk immersed himself in the study of rocket science and space exploration, devouring textbooks and consulting experts to gain a deep understanding of the field. Similarly, Musk's passion for electric vehicles led him to study automotive engineering and battery technology, laying the foundation for the development of Tesla's groundbreaking electric cars.

Pillar 4: Application - Transforming Knowledge into Action

Armed with his knowledge and insights, Musk applied innovative thinking and strategic execution to revolutionize multiple industries. At SpaceX, Musk's vision of making space travel affordable and accessible drove the development of the Falcon 1, Falcon 9, and Falcon Heavy rockets, which have become the backbone of commercial spaceflight. Similarly, at Tesla, Musk's relentless pursuit of sustainable transportation led to the development of the Model S, Model 3, Model X, and Model Y electric vehicles, setting new standards for performance and efficiency.

Pillar 5: Appreciation - Cultivating Recognition and Acknowledgment

As a leader, Musk understands the importance of appreciation in fostering a positive and collaborative work environment. He values the contributions of his team members and actively recognizes their efforts in advancing the company's mission. Musk's leadership style emphasizes transparency, accountability, and open communication, creating a culture where employees feel valued and empowered to innovate. Additionally, Musk regularly expresses gratitude to Tesla customers and SpaceX supporters, acknowledging their role in driving the company's success.

Pillar 6: Compensation - Recognizing and Rewarding Contributions

Musk believes in recognizing and rewarding the contributions of individuals to the success of his ventures. At SpaceX and Tesla, he has implemented innovative compensation structures, including performance-based bonuses and stock options, to incentivize employees and align their interests with the company's goals. Musk's approach to compensation emphasizes fairness, equity, and meritocracy, rewarding employees based on their contributions to the company's growth and success.

Pillar 7: Celebration - Culminating in Joyous Acknowledgment

Throughout his career, Musk has celebrated the achievements and milestones of his companies with enthusiasm and optimism. From the successful launch of SpaceX's Falcon rockets to the delivery of Tesla's first mass-market electric car, Musk has marked significant occasions with speeches, events, and social media posts, expressing gratitude to employees, customers, and supporters. Musk's celebratory spirit fosters a sense of camaraderie and shared accomplishment among stakeholders, inspiring continued innovation and success.

Elon Musk's life and journey exemplify the seven pillars of achievement, from his identification of opportunities to his transformative impact on multiple industries. Through vision, action, and a relentless pursuit of ambitious goals, Musk has revolutionized the fields of technology, transportation, and space exploration, leaving an indelible mark on the world. As he continues to push the boundaries of innovation and exploration, Musk's legacy will endure as a testament to the power of visionary leadership and the limitless potential of human ingenuity.

Michael Jordan: The Journey to Greatness

Michael Jordan, widely regarded as the greatest basketball player of all time, embodies the essence of achievement. His life story is a testament to the power of determination, resilience, and unwavering commitment to excellence. Through the lens of the seven pillars of achievement, we explore Jordan's remarkable journey from humble beginnings to global icon, highlighting the pivotal moments and guiding principles that shaped his legendary career on and off the court.

Pillar 1: Identification - Unveiling the Essence

Michael Jeffrey Jordan was born on February 17, 1963, in Brooklyn, New York, and raised in Wilmington, North Carolina. From a young age, Jordan displayed an unparalleled passion and talent for basketball. Despite facing numerous challenges and setbacks, including being cut from his high school varsity team as a sophomore, Jordan remained undeterred in his pursuit of greatness. He used rejection as fuel to propel himself forward, identifying his love for the game as the driving force behind his ambitions.

Pillar 2: Action - Bridging Vision and Reality

Driven by his vision of becoming the best basketball player in the world, Jordan took relentless action to turn his dreams into reality. He devoted countless hours to honing his skills, practicing long after his teammates had gone home. Jordan's unparalleled work ethic and dedication to his craft set him apart from his peers, laying the foundation for his future success. His relentless pursuit of excellence fueled his rise to prominence, culminating in a record-breaking career marked by six NBA championships and five MVP awards.

Pillar 3: Education - Empowering Through Knowledge

While Jordan's formal education centered on his academic pursuits, his true education came from the lessons learned on the basketball court. He absorbed knowledge from his coaches, teammates, and opponents, constantly seeking ways to improve and evolve as a player. Jordan's insatiable appetite for learning and his willingness to adapt to new challenges enabled him to stay ahead of the competition and redefine the game of basketball. His deep understanding of the intricacies of the sport empowered him to make split-second decisions and execute game-changing plays with precision.

Pillar 4: Application - Transforming Knowledge into Action

Armed with his knowledge and skills, Jordan applied his talents with unmatched precision and finesse on the basketball court. He possessed an innate ability to execute under pressure, rising to the occasion when his team needed him most. Jordan's competitive drive and unwavering focus made him a formidable opponent, capable of single-handedly dominating games and carrying his team to victory. His ability to translate his training and preparation into on-court success solidified his reputation as a basketball legend and cemented his place in sports history.

Pillar 5: Appreciation - Cultivating Recognition and Acknowledgment

Throughout his illustrious career, Jordan never lost sight of the importance of appreciation and recognition. He understood the value of acknowledging the contributions of his teammates, coaches, and fans, recognizing that success is a collective effort. Jordan expressed gratitude for the support he received throughout his journey, whether it was from his family, friends, or the countless fans who cheered him on from the stands. His humility and graciousness in victory and defeat endeared him to millions of people around the world, earning him the respect and admiration of his peers and fans alike.

Pillar 6: Compensation - Recognizing and Rewarding Contributions

As one of the most successful athletes of all time, Jordan's contributions to the game of basketball are immeasurable. He revolutionized the sport with his unparalleled athleticism, creativity, and competitive spirit, inspiring a generation of players to strive for greatness. Jordan's impact transcended the court, as he became a global icon and cultural phenomenon. His influence extended beyond basketball, as he leveraged his platform to advocate for social justice, philanthropy, and community empowerment. Jordan's legacy as a player, businessman, and philanthropist continues to shape the world around us, leaving an indelible mark on the fabric of society.

Pillar 7: Celebration - Culminating in Joyous Acknowledgment

Jordan's illustrious career is a testament to the power of celebration and joyous acknowledgment. He relished the opportunity to compete at the highest level and savor the fruits of his labor. Jordan celebrated his victories with humility and grace, always mindful of the sacrifices and dedication required to achieve success. Whether it was winning championships with his teammates or receiving accolades and honors for his individual achievements, Jordan never took his success for granted. He embraced each moment with gratitude and appreciation, cherishing the memories and experiences that defined his legendary career.

Michael Jordan's journey to greatness exemplifies the seven pillars of achievement, from his unwavering determination to his relentless pursuit of excellence. Through his remarkable career, Jordan inspired millions of people around the world to dream big, work hard, and never give up on their goals. His legacy as a basketball icon, entrepreneur, and philanthropist continues to inspire future generations to reach for the stars and strive for greatness in all aspects of their lives. As we reflect on Jordan's incredible achievements, we are reminded of the transformative power of perseverance, passion, and the relentless pursuit of excellence.

Edson Arantes do Nascimento – Pele: The Journey of a Football Legend

Edson Arantes do Nascimento, better known as Pele, is widely regarded as one of the greatest football players of all time. His extraordinary journey from a young boy in Brazil to a global sporting icon is a testament to the power of talent, determination, and resilience. Through the lens of the seven pillars of achievement, we explore Pele's remarkable life story, highlighting the key moments and guiding principles that shaped his legendary career on and off the football pitch.

Pillar 1: Identification - Unveiling the Essence

Pele was born on October 23, 1940, in Três Corações, Brazil. From a young age, he displayed an innate talent for football, honing his skills on the streets of Bauru. Pele's father, a former football player himself, recognized his son's potential and encouraged him to pursue his passion for the game. It was during this formative period that Pele identified football as his true calling, setting the stage for his extraordinary journey to greatness.

Pillar 2: Action - Bridging Vision and Reality

Determined to fulfill his dream of becoming a professional footballer, Pele took relentless action to turn his aspirations into reality. He devoted countless hours to practicing and perfecting his craft, often using makeshift balls and playing barefoot on the streets of his hometown. Pele's unwavering commitment to his goal propelled him forward, and at the age of 15, he was recruited by the renowned Brazilian club Santos FC. From there, his career soared to new heights as he rose through the ranks to become one of the most celebrated footballers of all time.

Pillar 3: Education - Empowering Through Knowledge

While Pele's formal education was limited, his true education came from the lessons learned on the football pitch. He absorbed knowledge from his coaches, teammates, and opponents, constantly seeking ways to improve and evolve as a player. Pele's deep understanding of the game enabled him to anticipate plays, read the field, and execute with precision. His ability to adapt to different playing styles and tactics made him a versatile and formidable opponent, capable of changing the course of a game with his unmatched skill and creativity.

Pillar 4: Application - Transforming Knowledge into Action

Armed with his knowledge and skills, Pele applied his talents with unparalleled precision and finesse on the football pitch. He possessed an innate ability to read the game and anticipate plays, making split-second decisions that left opponents stunned. Pele's remarkable athleticism, combined with his technical prowess and strategic vision, made him a dominant force in the world of football. His ability to translate his training and preparation into on-field success solidified his reputation as a football legend and earned him numerous accolades and honors throughout his illustrious career.

Pillar 5: Appreciation - Cultivating Recognition and Acknowledgment

Throughout his career, Pele remained humble and gracious, always acknowledging the contributions of his teammates, coaches, and fans. He understood that success in football was a team effort and made a point to express gratitude for the support he received throughout his journey. Pele's humility and sportsmanship endeared him to fans around the world, earning him the respect and admiration of his peers and opponents alike. He recognized that football was more than just a game; it was a unifying force that brought people together and transcended cultural and national boundaries.

Pillar 6: Compensation - Recognizing and Rewarding Contributions

As one of the most successful footballers in history, Pele's contributions to the game are immeasurable. He revolutionized the sport with his electrifying playing style, scoring goals with unprecedented precision and flair. Pele's impact extended beyond the football pitch, as he used his platform to advocate for social causes and promote peace and unity through sport. His legacy as a player, ambassador, and humanitarian continues to inspire millions of people around the world, leaving an indelible mark on the world of football and society as a whole.

Pillar 7: Celebration - Culminating in Joyous Acknowledgment

Pele's illustrious career was marked by countless moments of celebration and joyous acknowledgment. From winning his first World Cup with Brazil in 1958 to his final match with the New York Cosmos in 1977, Pele's achievements were met with cheers, applause, and adulation from fans around the world. He celebrated his victories with humility and grace, always mindful of the sacrifices and dedication required to achieve success. Pele's infectious smile and boundless enthusiasm endeared him to fans of all ages, making him a beloved and iconic figure in the world of football.

Pele's journey to greatness exemplifies the seven pillars of achievement, from his humble beginnings to his meteoric rise to stardom. Through talent, determination, and unwavering commitment, he transcended the sport of football and became a global icon and ambassador for the game. As we reflect on Pele's remarkable achievements, we are reminded of the transformative power of perseverance, passion, and the relentless pursuit of excellence. His legacy continues to inspire future generations of footballers and serves as a testament to the enduring impact of one man's dream to change the world through the beautiful game.

Martin Luther King Jr.: A Journey of Leadership and Legacy

Martin Luther King Jr., a towering figure in the civil rights movement, dedicated his life to the pursuit of justice, equality, and peace. Born on January 15, 1929, in Atlanta, Georgia, King's unwavering commitment to nonviolent activism and his powerful oratory skills made him a transformative leader whose legacy continues to inspire generations. Through the lens of the seven pillars of achievement, we explore King's extraordinary life journey, highlighting the key moments and guiding principles that shaped his legacy as a champion of civil rights and social justice.

Pillar 1: Identification - Unveiling the Essence

From a young age, Martin Luther King Jr. was acutely aware of the injustices and inequalities faced by African Americans in the United States. Growing up in the segregated South, he witnessed firsthand the pervasive effects of racial discrimination and prejudice. King's early experiences with racism instilled in him a deep sense of empathy and a fervent desire to challenge the status quo. As a student at Morehouse College, King grappled with the question of how he could contribute to the fight for racial equality, ultimately recognizing his calling to advocate for social change through nonviolent resistance.

Pillar 2: Action - Bridging Vision and Reality

Inspired by the teachings of Mahatma Gandhi and the principles of nonviolent protest, Martin Luther King Jr. emerged as a charismatic leader and spokesperson for the civil rights movement. He galvanized millions of Americans to take action against racial injustice through peaceful demonstrations, marches, and boycotts. King's leadership during the Montgomery Bus Boycott in 1955 catapulted him to national prominence, signaling the beginning of a new era in the struggle for civil rights. Despite facing threats, intimidation, and violence, King remained steadfast in his commitment to nonviolent protest, believing that love and justice would ultimately triumph over hatred and oppression.

Pillar 3: Education - Empowering Through Knowledge

Throughout his life, Martin Luther King Jr. emphasized the importance of education as a means of empowering individuals and communities. He believed that knowledge was a powerful tool for social change, enabling people to challenge existing norms and advocate for their rights. King's own academic achievements, including earning a Ph.D. in theology from Boston University, exemplified his commitment to lifelong learning and intellectual growth. He used his platform as a scholar and educator to disseminate his ideas and inspire others to join the struggle for equality and justice.

Pillar 4: Application - Transforming Knowledge into Action

Armed with his knowledge of nonviolent resistance and his deep understanding of the principles of justice and equality, Martin Luther King Jr. applied his teachings with strategic precision in the fight for civil rights. He organized and led numerous campaigns and protests, including the historic March on Washington for Jobs and Freedom in 1963, where he delivered his iconic "I Have a Dream" speech. King's ability to mobilize grassroots support and mobilize public opinion through peaceful protest was instrumental in advancing the cause of civil rights and bringing about legislative change, such as the passage of the Civil Rights Act of 1964 and the Voting Rights Act of 1965.

Pillar 5: Appreciation - Cultivating Recognition and Acknowledgment

Throughout his activism, Martin Luther King Jr. emphasized the importance of acknowledging and appreciating the contributions of others in the struggle for civil rights. He frequently expressed gratitude to the countless individuals, both known and unknown, who participated in marches, sit-ins, and boycotts, often at great personal risk. King understood that the success of the civil rights movement depended on the collective efforts of ordinary people committed to justice and equality. He celebrated their courage, resilience, and determination, recognizing that their sacrifices paved the way for progress and social change.

Pillar 6: Compensation - Recognizing and Rewarding Contributions

While Martin Luther King Jr. did not seek personal gain or recognition for his activism, he understood the importance of acknowledging and rewarding the contributions of others in the movement. He worked tirelessly to ensure that activists and organizers received the recognition and support they deserved, whether through public acknowledgment, financial assistance, or leadership opportunities. King's commitment to compensating and empowering grassroots leaders and organizers helped to sustain the momentum of the civil rights movement and foster a sense of solidarity and collective purpose among its participants.

Pillar 7: Celebration - Culminating in Joyous Acknowledgment

Martin Luther King Jr. believed that the struggle for civil rights was ultimately a celebration of the inherent dignity and worth of every individual. He envisioned a future where people of all races, religions, and backgrounds could come together in harmony and unity, celebrating their diversity and shared humanity. King's dream of a beloved community, where justice and equality prevailed, continues to inspire people around the world to work towards a better, more inclusive society. Though King's life was tragically cut short by an assassin's bullet in 1968, his vision of a world free from hatred and prejudice lives on, reminding us of the power of hope.

Colin Powell: A Journey of Leadership and Legacy

Colin Powell, a distinguished military leader, diplomat, and statesman, is a figure of immense influence and inspiration. Born on April 5, 1937, in Harlem, New York City, Powell rose to prominence through his remarkable achievements in the United States Army, where he became the first African American to serve as Chairman of the Joint Chiefs of Staff and later as Secretary of State. Through the lens of the seven pillars of achievement, we explore Powell's extraordinary life journey, highlighting the key moments and guiding principles that shaped his legacy as a leader and trailblazer.

Pillar 1: Identification - Unveiling the Essence

Colin Powell's journey towards achievement began with a deep sense of awareness and self-discovery. Growing up in the racially segregated neighborhoods of New York City, Powell faced numerous challenges and obstacles. However, he remained undeterred in his pursuit of excellence. Powell identified his passion for leadership and service at an early age, inspired by the examples set by his parents and mentors. He recognized the importance of education and hard work in overcoming adversity and charting a path towards success.

Pillar 2: Action - Bridging Vision and Reality

Armed with a clear vision of his goals, Colin Powell took decisive action to pursue his dreams. He excelled academically, earning a commission as a second lieutenant in the United States Army after graduating from the City College of New York. Powell's military career spanned over three decades, during which he distinguished himself as a capable and visionary leader. He rose through the ranks, demonstrating strategic acumen, integrity, and a commitment to excellence in every role he undertook.

Pillar 3: Education - Empowering Through Knowledge

Education played a pivotal role in Colin Powell's journey of achievement. He understood the transformative power of knowledge and lifelong learning. Powell pursued advanced degrees in military science and international relations, honing his expertise in strategic planning and diplomacy. He embraced opportunities for professional development, attending prestigious military schools and leadership programs. Powell's dedication to education empowered him to navigate complex challenges with confidence and competence.

Pillar 4: Application - Transforming Knowledge into Action

Colin Powell's ability to translate knowledge into action set him apart as a leader of exceptional caliber. He applied his expertise in military strategy and diplomacy to tackle some of the most pressing issues facing the nation. As Chairman of the Joint Chiefs of Staff, Powell played a central role in shaping U.S. military policy during the Gulf War, demonstrating strategic leadership and effective decision-making. His pragmatic approach to problem-solving and crisis management earned him widespread respect and admiration.

Pillar 5: Appreciation - Cultivating Recognition and Acknowledgment

Throughout his career, Colin Powell remained grounded in humility and gratitude. He recognized the contributions of his fellow soldiers, diplomats, and colleagues, attributing his success to their collective efforts. Powell's inclusive leadership style and ability to foster collaboration were instrumental in building cohesive teams and achieving shared objectives. He valued diversity and inclusion, recognizing the importance of respecting differing perspectives and harnessing the strengths of individuals from diverse backgrounds.

Pillar 6: Compensation - Recognizing and Rewarding Contributions

Colin Powell believed in the importance of recognizing and rewarding excellence. He advocated for merit-based promotions and opportunities for advancement, ensuring that talented individuals were given the recognition and support they deserved. Powell mentored and mentored countless aspiring leaders, empowering them to reach their full potential. He understood that investing in people was key to building a strong and resilient organization.

Pillar 7: Celebration - Culminating in Joyous Acknowledgment

Colin Powell's journey of achievement was marked by moments of celebration and reflection. He took pride in the accomplishments of his teams and celebrated their victories with humility and grace. Powell's leadership style was characterized by a genuine appreciation for the dedication and hard work of those around him. He understood that success was a collective effort and took joy in sharing achievements with others.

Colin Powell's life and legacy exemplify the principles of the seven pillars of achievement. From his humble beginnings in Harlem to his rise as a global statesman, Powell embodied the values of integrity, leadership, and service. His remarkable journey serves as a testament to the power of determination, resilience, and a commitment to excellence. As we reflect on his life and legacy, let us draw inspiration from Colin Powell's example and strive to emulate his principles of achievement in our own lives.

The Beatles: A Musical Odyssey

The Beatles, an iconic British rock band formed in Liverpool in 1960, revolutionized the music industry and left an indelible mark on popular culture. Comprising John Lennon, Paul McCartney, George Harrison, and Ringo Starr, the Beatles achieved unparalleled success and acclaim, becoming one of the best-selling music artists of all time. Through the lens of the seven pillars of achievement, we embark on a journey through the remarkable story of the Beatles, highlighting the key moments and guiding principles that propelled them to legendary status.

Pillar 1: Identification - Unveiling the Essence

The journey of the Beatles began with a shared passion for music and a relentless drive to succeed.

John Lennon and Paul McCartney, childhood friends with a shared love for rock and roll, recognized their musical chemistry and embarked on a journey to pursue their musical ambitions. Inspired by the sounds of American artists like Elvis Presley and Chuck Berry, the Beatles identified their unique musical style and set out to make their mark on the world.

Pillar 2: Action - Bridging Vision and Reality

Armed with their musical talents and unwavering determination, the Beatles took decisive action to achieve their goals. They honed their craft through countless hours of practice and performance, playing in clubs and pubs across Liverpool and Hamburg. Their relentless work ethic and commitment to excellence set them apart, earning them a loyal following and catching the attention of record labels. With a clear vision of their musical aspirations, the Beatles seized every opportunity to showcase their talent and propel their careers forward.

Pillar 3: Education - Empowering Through Knowledge

Education played a crucial role in the Beatles' journey of achievement, as they continuously sought to expand their musical horizons and refine their skills. Drawing inspiration from a diverse range of musical influences, from rock and roll to rhythm and blues, the Beatles embraced opportunities for musical experimentation and innovation. They studied the works of other artists, learned new techniques, and pushed the boundaries of traditional songwriting and recording methods. Through their relentless pursuit of musical knowledge, the Beatles transformed themselves into trailblazing pioneers of the music industry.

Pillar 4: Application - Transforming Knowledge into Action

The Beatles' ability to translate their musical knowledge into action was a key factor in their unprecedented success. With each new album, they pushed the boundaries of creativity and innovation, experimenting with new sounds, instruments, and recording techniques. From the infectious melodies of "She Loves You" to the psychedelic sounds of "Sgt. Pepper's Lonely Hearts Club Band," the Beatles demonstrated a remarkable ability to adapt and evolve, constantly reinventing themselves and captivating audiences around the world.

Pillar 5: Appreciation - Cultivating Recognition and Acknowledgment

Throughout their career, the Beatles remained grounded in humility and gratitude, acknowledging the contributions of their fellow musicians, producers, and collaborators. They valued the importance of teamwork and collaboration, recognizing that their success was built on the collective efforts of many. Whether in the studio or on stage, the Beatles fostered a culture of appreciation and respect, celebrating the talents of those around them and acknowledging their role in shaping their sound and success.

Pillar 6: Compensation - Recognizing and Rewarding Contributions

While financial compensation was certainly a factor in the Beatles' journey of achievement, their greatest rewards came from the creative fulfillment and artistic satisfaction they derived from their work. They took pride in their musical accomplishments and the impact their music had on millions of fans around the world. The Beatles' success was not measured solely in record sales or chart positions but in the lasting legacy of their music and the profound influence they had on generations of musicians and music lovers.

Pillar 7: Celebration - Culminating in Joyous Acknowledgment

The Beatles' journey of achievement was marked by countless moments of celebration and joyous acknowledgment. From their triumphant performances at iconic venues like Shea Stadium and the Ed Sullivan Show to their induction into the Rock and Roll Hall of Fame, the Beatles celebrated their achievements with humility and gratitude. They took joy in sharing their music with the world and were grateful for the unwavering support of their fans, whose love and appreciation fueled their passion for music.

The Beatles' story is a testament to the power of passion, perseverance, and collaboration in achieving greatness. Through their unwavering commitment to their craft and their ability to embody the seven pillars of achievement, the Beatles transcended the boundaries of music and left an enduring legacy that continues to inspire and captivate audiences to this day. As we reflect on their remarkable journey, let us celebrate the enduring legacy of the Beatles and the timeless music that continues to bring joy and inspiration to millions around the world.

Bob Marley: A Musical Odyssey

Bob Marley, the legendary reggae musician and cultural icon, left an indelible mark on the world with his music and message of peace, love, and unity. Born on February 6, 1945, in Nine Mile, Jamaica, Marley rose from humble beginnings to become one of the most influential figures in music history. Through the lens of the seven pillars of achievement, we embark on a journey through the remarkable life and career of Bob Marley, exploring the key moments and guiding principles that propelled him to greatness.

Pillar 1: Identification - Unveiling the Essence

Bob Marley's journey of achievement began with a deep understanding of his cultural heritage and a profound connection to the music of Jamaica. Growing up in the rural village of Nine Mile, Marley was immersed in the rhythms of reggae and the messages of Rastafarianism from an early age. He recognized the power of music as a tool for social change and self-expression, and he embraced his role as a messenger of hope and unity for his people.

Pillar 2: Action - Bridging Vision and Reality

Armed with his vision of spreading a message of love and unity through music, Bob Marley took decisive action to pursue his goals. He formed the band The Wailers with childhood friends Peter Tosh and Bunny Wailer, and together they began to make their mark on the Jamaican music scene. With their revolutionary blend of reggae, ska, and rocksteady, the Wailers captured the hearts of audiences and set the stage for Marley's ascent to international stardom.

Pillar 3: Education - Empowering Through Knowledge

Education played a crucial role in Bob Marley's journey, as he sought to deepen his understanding of music, culture, and spirituality. Marley drew inspiration from a diverse range of influences, from the teachings of Rastafarianism to the music of artists like Curtis Mayfield and Bob Dylan. He immersed himself in the history and traditions of Jamaica, studying the rhythms of reggae and the social and political issues facing his country. Through his lifelong quest for knowledge, Marley empowered himself to become a voice for the voiceless and a beacon of hope for the oppressed.

Pillar 4: Application - Transforming Knowledge into Action

Bob Marley's ability to translate his knowledge and vision into action was a defining characteristic of his success. With each new song, he tackled pressing social and political issues, from poverty and inequality to racism and oppression. Marley used his music as a platform for change, spreading messages of love, unity, and liberation to audiences around the world. Through his powerful lyrics and soul-stirring melodies, Marley inspired millions to stand up for justice and equality, turning his ideals into tangible realities.

Pillar 5: Appreciation - Cultivating Recognition and Acknowledgment

Throughout his career, Bob Marley remained grounded in humility and gratitude, acknowledging the contributions of his fellow musicians and collaborators. He valued the importance of teamwork and collaboration, recognizing that his success was built on the collective efforts of many. Marley expressed his appreciation for his bandmates, producers, and supporters, celebrating their talents and contributions to his music and message.

Pillar 6: Compensation - Recognizing and Rewarding Contributions

While financial compensation was certainly a factor in Bob Marley's journey, his greatest rewards came from the impact his music had on the world. Marley took pride in using his platform to uplift and empower others, and he considered the love and appreciation of his fans to be the greatest reward of all. Through his music, Marley sought to enrich the lives of others and create positive change in the world, and his legacy continues to inspire generations of musicians and activists to this day.

Pillar 7: Celebration - Culminating in Joyous Acknowledgment

Bob Marley's journey of achievement was marked by countless moments of celebration and joyous acknowledgment. From sold-out concerts to international acclaim, Marley's music brought people together in celebration of love, unity, and freedom. He reveled in the joy of performing for his fans and took pride in the impact his music had on the world. Though Marley's life was cut short by cancer at the age of 36, his legacy lives on through his timeless music and enduring message of hope and redemption.

Bob Marley's life and legacy serve as a testament to the power of music to inspire change and unite people across cultures and continents. Through his unwavering commitment to his ideals and his relentless pursuit of excellence, Marley embodied the seven pillars of achievement and left an indelible mark on the world. As we reflect on his remarkable journey, let us celebrate the life and music of Bob Marley and honor his enduring legacy of peace, love, and unity.

WORDS OF SUCCESS

These are the list of words mentioned in this book that will enable you to appreciate and apply to your personal and professional endeavors.

1. Achievement: The successful accomplishment of a goal or task.
2. Blueprint: A detailed plan or strategy for achieving a specific objective.
3. Success: The attainment of desired outcomes or goals.
4. Pillars: Fundamental principles or components that support a structure or system.
5. Identification: The process of recognizing or discerning challenges, opportunities, or goals.
6. Action: Taking steps or initiatives to move toward desired objectives or outcomes.
7. Education: Continuous learning and knowledge acquisition to enhance skills and understanding.
8. Application: The practical implementation or use of acquired knowledge or insights.
9. Appreciation: Recognition and acknowledgment of efforts, contributions, or achievements.
10. Compensation: Reward or recognition for contributions or achievements, often beyond monetary value.

11. Celebration: Commemoration or acknowledgment of successes, milestones, or achievements.
12. Purpose: A sense of direction or intention that guides actions and decisions.
13. Strategy: A plan of action designed to achieve a specific goal or objective.
14. Innovation: Introducing new ideas, methods, or products to drive progress and improvement.
15. Resilience: The ability to adapt and bounce back from challenges or setbacks.
16. Motivation: The driving force or incentive that prompts action or behavior.
17. Persistence: Continued effort or determination in the face of obstacles or difficulties.
18. Commitment: Dedication or loyalty to a cause, goal, or relationship.
19. Collaboration: Working together with others to achieve common goals or objectives.
20. Leadership: Guiding and inspiring others to achieve collective goals or visions.
21. Vision: A clear and inspiring picture of the desired future state or outcome.
22. Integrity: Acting with honesty, ethics, and moral principles in all endeavors.
23. Empowerment: Giving individuals or groups the authority, resources, or confidence to take action and make decisions.

24. Adaptability: The ability to adjust or modify approaches in response to changing circumstances.
25. Synergy: The combined effect of collaboration or cooperation that produces greater results than individual efforts.
26. Reflection: Thoughtful consideration or contemplation of experiences, actions, or outcomes.
27. Gratitude: A feeling of thankfulness or appreciation for blessings, opportunities, or support.
28. Self-awareness: Understanding one's own emotions, strengths, weaknesses, and motivations.
29. Feedback: Constructive input or commentary provided to improve performance, products, or processes.
30. Growth mindset: Believing that abilities and intelligence can be developed through effort, learning, and perseverance.
31. Initiative: Taking proactive action or responsibility to address challenges or opportunities.
32. Empathy: Understanding and sharing the feelings, perspectives, or experiences of others.
33. Teamwork: Collaborating effectively with others to achieve shared goals or objectives.
34. Accountability: Taking ownership and responsibility for one's actions, decisions, or outcomes.

35. Adaptation: Adjusting to changes in the environment, circumstances, or expectations.
36. Problem-solving: Finding solutions to challenges or obstacles through analysis, creativity, and critical thinking.
37. Communication: Sharing information, ideas, or feedback effectively with others.
38. Focus: Concentrating attention and effort on priorities or objectives.
39. Time management: Organizing and prioritizing tasks or activities to maximize productivity and efficiency.
40. Balance: Maintaining harmony or equilibrium between different aspects of life, such as work and personal life.
41. Patience: Remaining calm and persevering through delays, difficulties, or setbacks.
42. Networking: Building and maintaining relationships with others for mutual support, collaboration, or opportunities.
43. Confidence: Belief in one's abilities, worth, or potential to succeed.
44. Decision-making: Evaluating options and choosing the best course of action to achieve desired outcomes.
45. Trust: Confidence in the reliability, integrity, or competence of others.
46. Influence: The ability to affect or persuade others' thoughts, feelings, or actions.
47. Empathy: Understanding and sharing the feelings, perspectives, or experiences of others.

48. Ambition: A strong desire or drive to achieve success, power, or recognition.
49. Courage: Acting in the face of fear, adversity, or uncertainty.
50. Discipline: Consistently following rules, routines, or plans to achieve goals.
51. Creativity: Generating novel ideas, solutions, or expressions through imagination and originality.
52. Adaptation: Adjusting to changes in the environment, circumstances, or expectations.
53. Tenacity: Persistence or determination in the pursuit of goals or objectives.
54. Curiosity: A strong desire to learn, explore, or understand new things.
55. Collaboration: Working together with others to achieve common goals or objectives.
56. Leadership: Guiding and inspiring others to achieve collective goals or visions.
57. Optimism: A positive outlook or attitude towards the future, even in the face of challenges.
58. Accountability: Taking ownership and responsibility for one's actions, decisions, or outcomes.
59. Flexibility: Willingness to adapt or modify plans, approaches, or perspectives in response to changing circumstances.
60. Integrity: Acting with honesty, ethics, and moral principles in all endeavors.

61. Passion: Strong enthusiasm, drive, or commitment towards a particular interest or goal.
62. Perseverance: Continued effort or determination in the face of obstacles or difficulties.
63. Resourcefulness: Finding creative or effective ways to solve problems or achieve goals with limited resources.
64. Empowerment: Giving individuals or groups the authority, resources, or confidence to take action and make decisions.
65. Open-mindedness: Willingness to consider new ideas, perspectives, or information without prejudice.
66. Self-discipline: The ability to control one's impulses, emotions, and behaviors to achieve desired outcomes.
67. Adaptability: Adjusting to changes in the environment, circumstances, or expectations.
68. Collaboration: Working together with others to achieve common goals or objectives.
69. Leadership: Guiding and inspiring others to achieve collective goals or visions.
70. Innovation: Introducing new ideas, methods, or products to drive progress and improvement.
71. Resilience: The ability to bounce back from setbacks, adversity, or challenges.
72. Motivation: The drive or desire to accomplish goals or fulfill aspirations.

73. Persistence: Continued effort or determination in the face of obstacles or setbacks.
74. Creativity: Thinking outside the box to generate new ideas, solutions, or approaches.
75. Problem-solving: Finding effective solutions to challenges or obstacles.
76. Communication: Sharing information, ideas, or feedback effectively with others.
77. Collaboration: Working together with others to achieve common goals or objectives.
78. Empathy: Understanding and sharing the feelings, perspectives, or experiences of others.
79. Adaptability: Adjusting to changes in the environment, circumstances, or expectations.
80. Critical thinking: Evaluating information, arguments, or ideas in a logical and systematic manner.
81. Decision-making: Making informed choices or judgments to achieve desired outcomes.
82. Time management: Organizing and prioritizing tasks or activities to maximize productivity and efficiency.
83. Goal-setting: Establishing clear and achievable objectives to work towards.
84. Leadership: Guiding and inspiring others to achieve collective goals or visions.
85. Teamwork: Collaborating effectively with others to achieve shared goals or objectives.
86. Confidence: Belief in one's abilities, worth, or potential to succeed.

87. Adaptation: Adjusting to changes in the environment, circumstances, or expectations.
88. Resilience: The ability to bounce back from setbacks, adversity, or challenges.
89. Persistence: Continued effort or determination in the face of obstacles or setbacks.
90. Innovation: Introducing new ideas, methods, or products to drive progress and improvement.
91. Problem-solving: Finding effective solutions to challenges or obstacles.
92. Communication: Sharing information, ideas, or feedback effectively with others.
93. Collaboration: Working together with others to achieve common goals or objectives.
94. Empathy: Understanding and sharing the feelings, perspectives, or experiences of others.
95. Adaptability: Adjusting to changes in the environment, circumstances, or expectations.
96. Critical thinking: Evaluating information, arguments, or ideas in a logical and systematic manner.
97. Decision-making: Making informed choices or judgments to achieve desired outcomes.
98. Time management: Organizing and prioritizing tasks or activities to maximize productivity and efficiency.
99. Goal-setting: Establishing clear and achievable objectives to work towards.

100.   Leadership: Guiding and inspiring others to achieve collective goals or visions.

50 WORLD'S GREATEST AUTHORS

These are the world's greatest authors and experts in the field of achievement, personal development, leadership, psychology and organizational behavior. Their work aligns with this body of work and contribution to higher education and society.

1. Carol S. Dweck - Known for her work on growth mindset and motivation.
2. John P. Kotter - Author of numerous books on leadership and organizational change.
3. Angela Duckworth - Renowned for her research on grit and perseverance.
4. Stephen R. Covey - Author of "The 7 Habits of Highly Effective People" focusing on personal development and effectiveness.
5. Daniel Goleman - Expert on emotional intelligence and its impact on leadership and success.
6. Mihaly Csikszentmihalyi - Known for his work on flow theory and optimal human experiences.
7. Simon Sinek - Author of "Start With Why," focusing on leadership and organizational culture.
8. Malcolm Gladwell - Renowned for his books exploring factors contributing to success, such as "Outliers."

9. Adam Grant - Expert on workplace dynamics, motivation, and organizational behavior.
10. Peter Senge - Known for his work on organizational learning and systems thinking.
11. Clayton M. Christensen - Author of "The Innovator's Dilemma," focusing on disruptive innovation.
12. Brene Brown - Known for her research on vulnerability, courage, and shame resilience.
13. Tony Robbins - Motivational speaker and author of numerous books on personal development and achievement.
14. Robert Kegan - Expert on adult development and constructive developmental theory.
15. Marshall Goldsmith - Renowned executive coach and author of books on leadership and personal development.
16. Nassim Nicholas Taleb - Known for his work on risk-taking, resilience, and anti-fragility.
17. Daniel Pink - Author of books on motivation, behavior, and the changing world of work.
18. Jim Collins - Renowned for his books on leadership and organizational excellence, such as "Good to Great."
19. Susan Cain - Expert on introversion and its impact on leadership and creativity.
20. Edgar H. Schein - Known for his work on organizational culture and leadership.
21. Teresa M. Amabile - Expert on creativity and motivation in the workplace.

22. Richard Boyatzis - Co-author of "Primal Leadership" and expert on emotional intelligence.
23. Peter F. Drucker - Renowned management consultant and author of numerous influential books on management and leadership.
24. Rosabeth Moss Kanter - Expert on innovation, leadership, and change management.
25. Gary Hamel - Known for his work on management innovation and organizational strategy.
26. Amy C. Edmondson - Expert on team dynamics, psychological safety, and learning organizations.
27. Charles Duhigg - Author of "The Power of Habit," focusing on the science of habit formation and change.
28. Barbara Kellerman - Expert on leadership studies and author of several influential books on leadership theory.
29. Patrick Lencioni - Known for his work on organizational health and team dynamics.
30. Gretchen Spreitzer - Expert on empowerment, resilience, and positive organizational scholarship.
31. Scott Barry Kaufman - Expert on creativity, intelligence, and human potential.
32. John C. Maxwell - Author of numerous books on leadership and personal growth.
33. Susan David - Renowned psychologist and author focusing on emotional agility.

34. Rosabeth Moss Kanter - Expert on innovation, leadership, and change management.
35. Robert B. Cialdini - Known for his work on influence and persuasion.
36. Charles Duhigg - Author of "The Power of Habit," exploring habits and behavior change.
37. Chip Heath and Dan Heath - Co-authors of books on decision-making, change, and organizational behavior.
38. Ellen Langer - Expert on mindfulness and the psychology of possibility.
39. Martin E.P. Seligman - Renowned for his work on positive psychology and well-being.
40. Sonja Lyubomirsky - Expert on happiness, positive emotions, and well-being.
41. David G. Myers - Psychologist known for his work on social psychology and well-being.
42. Albert Bandura - Pioneering psychologist known for his work on self-efficacy and social learning theory.
43. Carol Ryff - Expert on psychological well-being and resilience.
44. Rick Hanson - Neuroscientist and author focusing on the science of happiness and resilience.
45. Ellen J. Langer - Expert on mindfulness and the psychology of possibility.
46. Adam Alter - Author and researcher focusing on behavioral economics and technology addiction.

47. Jonathan Haidt - Psychologist known for his work on morality, happiness, and well-being.
48. Martin E.P. Seligman - Renowned for his work on positive psychology and flourishing.
49. Robert J. Sternberg - Psychologist known for his research on intelligence, creativity, and wisdom.
50. Carol Tavris - Expert on cognitive dissonance, human behavior, and social psychology.

ABOUT THE AUTHOR

Dr. Lester Reid stands as a towering figure in the realms of education, business consultancy, financial management and personal development. With a critical background spanning over two decades, Dr. Reid has left an indelible mark as a transformational speaker, educator, author, and executive consultant. His journey towards excellence is marked by an impressive array of qualifications and experiences, reflecting his relentless pursuit of knowledge and expertise.

As a seasoned academic, Dr. Reid holds a plethora of degrees from prestigious institutions, including an Executive DBA in Accounting from West Virginia University, Doctor of Business Administration in

Management from Grand Canyon University, Master of Taxation from Mississippi State University, Master of Science in Accounting, Master of Science in Management, and MBA from Texas A&M University, Commerce, Master of Education in Adult and Higher Education from the University of Houston among others. This extensive academic foundation serves as the bedrock upon which his professional prowess stands.

A certified Six Sigma Black Belt, as well as holding certifications in Yellow, Green, and White Belts. Dr. Reid exemplifies a commitment to operational excellence and efficiency. His expertise in process improvement methodologies adds another dimension to his already impressive skill set, allowing him to drive tangible results in organizational settings.

Dr. Reid's literary contributions further solidify his status as a thought leader and influencer. His books, which range from Amazon best sellers to #1 hot new releases, serve as invaluable resources for individuals seeking personal and professional development. Through his writing, Dr. Reid imparts wisdom, motivation, and inspiration, guiding readers towards realizing their full potential.

Beyond his academic and professional achievements, Dr. Reid is deeply passionate about fostering continual human development. He firmly believes that personal growth and professional expertise are the cornerstones of economic and financial success. As such, he dedicates himself to teaching and training doctoral students, executives, graduates, and undergraduates, empowering them to excel in their respective fields.

Dr. Lester Reid's journey embodies the essence of lifelong learning, resilience, and dedication. His unwavering commitment to excellence, coupled with his vast expertise and profound insights, continues to inspire and empower countless individuals and organizations on their paths to success.

www.ingramcontent.com/pod-product-compliance
Lightning Source LLC
Chambersburg PA
CBHW032302210326
41520CB00047B/902